Expert Litemanship

Expert Lifemanship

MASTERING THE ART OF LIVING

Text by Warren Wiersbe

Photographs and Captions by Ken Jenkins

CLC PUBLICATIONS

Fort Washington, PA 19034

Expert Lifemanship
ISBN: 978-0-87508-988-1
Copyright 2008 CLC Publications

This printing 2008

Published by CLC Publications

U.S.A.
P.O. Box 1449, Fort Washington, PA 19034

GREAT BRITAIN
51 The Dean, Alresford, Hants, SO24 9BJ

AUSTRALIA
P.O. Box 2299, Strathpine, QLD 4500

NEW ZEALAND
10 MacArthur Street, Feilding

Unless otherwise indicated, Scripture quotations are from
The English Standard Version, copyright 2001 by Crossway Bibles.
Wheaton, Illinois, a division of Good News Publishers.

To my wife, Vicki, always by my side.

As Vance Havner wrote,

"Whatever the weather, we'll weather the weather, whether we like it or not."

Ken

Even youths shall faint and be weary, and young men shall fall exhausted; but they who wait for the LORD shall renew their strength; they shall mount up with wings like eagles; they shall run and not be weary; they shall walk and not faint. (Isa. 40:30–31)

Contents

As if to signify the source of its strength, the magnificent eagle stands with outstretched wings, catching the wind force that will carry it to greater heights.

Living

"L' Chaim! L'Chaim!"

This joyful traditional Hebrew expression (you may remember it from *Fiddler on the Roof*) sometimes comes to mind when I encounter a tough situation or when I learn that another long-time friend has passed into eternity. "To life! To life! L'Chaim!"

"I have a fatal disease," wrote a pessimistic wit. "It's called life. You can't get out of it without dying." To which our Jewish friends would reply, "L'Chaim! To life!" It makes a difference when you face life with faith and anticipation instead of with doubt and fear.

This book is about learning to view life as a gift of God. Its theme is not how to make a living, but how to make a *life*. The focus is on values and character, not prices and reputation. If we take care of the values and character, the prices and reputation will take care of themselves.

Most people have a mental picture—a metaphor—of what they think life really is. When he wrote the Declaration of Independence, Thomas Jefferson called it "an unalienable right," along with liberty and the pursuit of happiness. Jefferson was thinking politically. The Yiddish writer Sholom Aleichem, whose stories supplied the plot for *Fiddler on the Roof*, once described life as "a blister on top of a tumor and a boil on top of that." He was thinking emotionally.

The American poet Carl Sandburg compared life to an onion—"you peel it off one layer at a time, and sometimes you weep." British poet John Masefield saw it as "a long headache in a noisy street," and British playwright George Bernard Shaw called it "a series of inspired follies." Is their choice of metaphors a key to their philosophy of life? Perhaps.

9

What life does to us depends a good deal on what life finds in us, and as the years march by, our views of life have a way of changing. When we feel weak and afraid, life becomes a dangerous battle. If we're weary and exhausted, it is a heavy burden, and when we can't seem to make the right decisions, it is a confusing maze. When our days move along with ease and enjoyment, then life is a party.

But when everything seems to be falling apart, life becomes an uncomfortable journey and we're not always sure where we're going. Sometimes we enjoy life and sometimes we just endure it and wish we could run away and hide. Even the great King David said, "Oh, that I had wings like a dove! I would fly away and be at rest" (Ps. 55:6). Unfortunately, some people even try to escape life and needlessly destroy themselves in the process.

One of the most helpful metaphors of human life is this: *Life is a gift*. We didn't ask to be born; life was given to us. Alfred P. Doolittle, father of Eliza Doolittle of *My Fair Lady* fame, made a wise statement when he said of his daughter, "I gave her the greatest gift of all—the gift of life." How else would she have gotten it? The scientist isn't sure what life is and the philosopher ponders what life means, but neither one has yet found all the answers.

But while they're wrestling with these profound mysteries, you and I still have to live and do it as successfully as possible. Most of the six billion-plus people on this globe pay little or no attention to these high-level discussions. Their greatest concerns are "Where can I get the next meal?" or "How can I find a new job?" or "What will happen if I can't pay my bills?" Pondering the philosophical is a luxury, but confronting the practical is a necessity. Life comes at us like a jet plane, day after day, minute by minute, and we have to face life and do something constructive with it.

Life is God's gift to us, and *what we do with life is our gift to Him*. Life is an undeserved stewardship for which we ought to give thanks, and we show our gratitude by giving Him our best. In these pages, we hope to share some practical suggestions about how this works. As we consider God's gift of life, we have to decide whether we're going to waste it, spend it or invest it.

It's foolish to waste life because nobody can live life over again and have a second chance. Yes, we can make new beginnings, and we should, but we can't change the past. It's a tragedy when people are successes at making a living but failures at making a life. Their houses are the envy of their friends, but their homes are in shambles. These people have great reputations but very little character. "For what does it profit a man to gain the whole world and forfeit his soul?" (Mark 8:36).

No, wasting one's life isn't the route to take, nor is merely spending one's life. Pity the people whose idea of life is to erase their individuality while they major on conforming to the world and pleasing the crowd. Each baby born is unique and has the right to grow up to fulfill his or her distinctive purpose in life. Human beings are not interchangeable parts in a great social machine, grinding away and becoming more and more nondescript every year. People are unique; they are alike but also different, just as flowers and trees are.

Because people are alike, they can work together and make a living. Because people are different, they can be themselves and make a unique life. Society isn't a machine; it's a living organism, and it takes both likenesses and differences to keep people and society healthy and creative. This means investing our lives individually in that for which the Lord put us here.

Some of the biblical metaphors for life help us better understand this gift and why we should invest it wisely. Job compared life to a breath (Job 7:7) and James calls it "a mist that appears for a little time and then vanishes" (James 4:14). An anonymous poet wrote, "For my days pass away like smoke" (Ps. 102:3), and Moses, Job, David and Isaiah all compared life to grass and flowers that appear and then quickly fade away (Ps. 90:3–6; Job 14:2; Ps. 103:15; Isa. 40:6–8). "The grass withers," wrote Isaiah, "the flower fades when the breath of the LORD blows on it…"

If life is like grass, flowers and smoke, then it is fragile and brief and its glory doesn't last. "For we are but of yesterday and know nothing," said Job's friend Bildad, "for our days on earth are a shadow" (Job 8:9). Life goes by all too quickly. As John Lennon put it, "Life is what happens when you're making other plans." Mark Twain wrote, "Fame is a vapor, popularity an accident; the only earthly certainty is oblivion." Twain was a bit of a pessimist and may have been having a bad day when he wrote that, but

Every bend in the trail leads to new expectation and delight every step forward represents accomplishment. The surroundings change but the direction remains the same—onward and upward!

there's a germ of truth in it.

Life is not only brief and fragile, it is also difficult. The Bible is very clear on that point and makes no attempt to disguise it. There are many pleasures in life, "but man is born to trouble as the sparks fly upward" (Job 5:7). Get acquainted with the "movers and shakers" in the Bible and in human history and you will discover that they had more than their share of tears and trials. Some of these problems they brought on themselves, as we all do at times; some were caused by others; and some were planned and sent by the Lord.

Psychiatrist Scott Peck begins his book *The Road Less Traveled* with, "Life is difficult." Then he adds, "Once we truly know that life is difficult—once we truly understand and accept it—then life is no longer difficult."[1] The difficulties haven't changed or disappeared, but *we* have changed and our outlook is more realistic. The Christian believer says, "Okay, if life is difficult, then I'll face it with faith and courage and with the Lord's help, I'll win some battles."

Life is hard because we live in a fallen world among people who, like us, are also fallen and infected with what the Bible calls sin. "For the creation was subjected to futility," explains the apostle Paul, but then he promises us that one day "the creation itself will be set free from its bondage to corruption and obtain the freedom of the glory of the children of God" (Rom. 8:20–21).

That word "futility" is reminiscent of Solomon's long sermon that begins, "Vanity of vanities, says the Preacher, vanity of vanities! All is vanity" (Eccles. 1:2). The Hebrew word translated "vanity" means "emptiness, vapor, that which vanishes quickly and leaves nothing behind." My Hebrew professor in seminary defined it as "that which is left when a soap bubble bursts." How sad it is when people devote their lives to chasing soap bubbles and, upon catching them, have nothing in their hands. "And the world is passing away along with its desires, but whoever does the will of God abides forever" (1 John 2:17).

Life is fragile and brief, life is difficult—but life is worth it! To grumble at life or try to escape it because of its difficulties is to miss all it really contains and what God has in store for those who trust Him.

"Few and evil have been the days of the years of my life," old Jacob told Pharaoh (Gen. 47:9), and he was speaking the truth; but while speaking his last words to his sons, Jacob cried out, "I wait for your salvation, O LORD" (Gen. 49:18). Paul demonstrated this same courage when he wrote, "For I consider that the sufferings of this present time are not worth comparing with the glory that is to be revealed to us" (Rom. 8:18). David had a difficult life as a father, a soldier and a ruler, and yet when the old shepherd looked back, he declared that goodness and mercy had followed him all the days of his life (Ps. 23:6). It was worth it all!

Life is God's gift to us and God's school for us. Moses had it right when he prayed, "So teach us to number our days that we may get a heart of wisdom" (Ps. 90:12). When difficulties come our way, we're prone to ask, "How can I get out of this?" when we ought to be asking, "What can I get out of this?"

We waste our opportunities to gain maturity and wisdom because we look for the easy way out. A heart of wisdom is gained by going through the struggle and receiving some bruises, not by sitting in the bleachers and cheering for others. "We won!" the spectators shout, but all they did was watch and make noise. It was the players and coaching staff on the field or the court that paid the price.

Life is a school in which we learn the most valuable lessons from the most difficult experiences. "It is better to go to the house of mourning than to go to the house of feasting," wrote King Solomon. "The heart of the wise is in the house of mourning, but the heart of fools is in the house of mirth" (Eccles. 7:2, 4).

This doesn't mean we must boycott parties and focus on funerals, because even Solomon admitted there's a right time for each of the varied experiences of life (Eccles. 3:1–8). Solomon simply means we should accept the tears as well as the laughter, the pain as well as the pleasure, and let them teach us the lessons we must learn as maturing people.

The rumble of thunder is brief, though it causes the ground to tremble. But like the morning mist, the clouds rise from the valley and fade away. Life's storms pass as we journey on.

The mother fox romps as the young kits observe and mimic her every move. The effort is exhausting, but vital to the growth of her young.

While we're on this earth, we never graduate from the school of life. However, we can make progress from one level to another—what Peter calls growing "in the grace and knowledge of our Lord and Savior Jesus Christ" (2 Pet. 3:18) and Paul describes as going "from one degree of glory to another" (2 Cor. 3:18). Even our Savior "learned obedience through what he suffered" (Heb. 5:8).

"So teach us to number our days" is what Moses prayed (Ps. 90:12). But very few people number their days; instead we number our years. Moses was 120 years old when he died, but each of those years was lived a day at a time. He told the people of Israel "as your days, so shall your strength be" (Deut. 33:25). Jacob used the interesting phrase "the days of the years of my sojourning" (Gen. 47:9).

Jesus instructed us to pray for "daily bread" and not to try to live two days at a time. "Therefore do not be anxious about tomorrow, for tomorrow will be anxious for itself. Sufficient for the day is its own trouble" (Matt. 6:34). An old bit of doggerel says, "Yard by yard life is hard, but inch by inch life's a cinch." We live a day at a time and seek by God's grace to carry each day's burdens and learn each day's lessons. That's an important step toward expert lifemanship.

While the Bible takes a serious view of life, it is not a negative view. In fact, Scripture assures us that God "richly provides us with everything to enjoy" (1 Tim. 6:17). Yes, life is fragile and brief; it is difficult, a school with a tough curriculum. But God wants His children to enjoy life, not in spite of their problems but *because* of them!

"When a woman is giving birth," Jesus told His disciples, "she has sorrow because her hour has come, but when she has delivered the baby, she no longer remembers the anguish, for joy that a human being has been born into the world" (John 16:21). The point our Lord was making is *the source of the pain also produced the joy!* The difficult situations of life can cause pain, but they are also pregnant with gladness; so let new life spring forth!

Each tree in the orchard is pruned by the trials of nature. Storms sweep the valley, and pests of all descriptions attack the new growth. Some trees stand firm, and in the time of harvest hang full and lovely with much fruit.

"For the moment all discipline seems painful rather than pleasant, but later it yields the peaceful fruit of righteousness to those who have been trained by it" (Heb. 12:11). So gather in the harvest! It has in it the seeds for more fruit.

The man who regards his own life and that of his fellow creatures as meaningless is not merely unhappy but hardly fit for life. – Albert Einstein

Young eaglets in the nest—fragile, defenseless and vulnerable—are completely dependent. Yet soon they will soar to amazing heights.

2 Trusting

The privilege of living must not be separated from the responsibility of trusting. Trust is the glue that holds life and society together—it keeps things going. The moment you were born, there were hands to receive you and provide for you, and you learned to trust them. As you grew, various influences watched over you, taught you and loved you. You learned to trust your parents, your siblings, your friends and your teachers. You were learning to live by faith.

As your knowledge and experience grew, you learned to evaluate people and circumstances and you discovered what to accept and what to avoid. Whether or not you consider yourself a "religious" person, your life was being held together by faith. It still is.

But there are two mistakes to avoid when it comes to this life of trust. First, don't look at trusting as a strange mystical experience for the elite. Trust is a very practical thing for everyone. It's the foundation for every human agreement and contract, from a signature on a credit card statement to the oath of office repeated by the President of the United States. Trust is the basis for friendship, citizenship and neighborliness. It often paves the way for love, and then, with love, becomes the basis for marriage. Whenever somebody betrays our trust, we're deeply hurt and we find it difficult to rebuild what was destroyed. Trust is a personal and practical experience that is at the heart of life itself, "for we walk by faith, not by sight" (2 Cor. 5:7).

The second mistake to avoid is thinking that Christian believers live by faith but that nobody else needs it. The difference isn't that the one trusts and the other one doesn't; the difference is the *object* of their faith. Everybody has faith in something or someone (if only in themselves or their checkbook), but Christian believers have faith in Jesus Christ, the Son of God. Your faith is only as good as its object.

Morning shafts of light signal a fresh beginning. The waking of a new day during the changing of seasons is a reminder of His unshakable faithfulness.

Trust money and you will get what money can give. Trust people and you will get what they can give. Trust the Lord, and you will get what God can give. Like Peter, Christians have confessed, "You are the Christ, the Son of the living God" (Matt. 16:16) and "You have the words of eternal life, and we have believed, and have come to know, that you are the Holy One of God" (John 6:68–69). Our faith in Christ is the power that energizes us and the compass that guides us. "Some trust in chariots and some in horses, but we trust in the name of the LORD our God" (Ps. 20:7).

Israel's deliverance from Babylon was the second "exodus" in the history of the Jewish people. The first, the exodus from Egypt under the leadership of the prophet Moses, involved one miracle after another (Exod. 1–15). The Lord had sent nine devastating plagues to Egypt, but Pharaoh still refused to submit to Him and let the people go. The tenth plague brought death to all of Egypt's firstborn, and it was this judgment that finally moved Pharaoh to allow the Jewish people to leave the country.

The Jewish firstborn were protected from death by the blood of a slain lamb applied to the doorframe of each house. This was a picture of Jesus Christ, the Lamb of God, who would one day die for the sins of the world (John 1:29). Then God opened up the Red Sea so the people of Israel could march out of Egypt into freedom.

Our Jewish friends celebrate Passover each spring and recall God's mercy in delivering them from slavery. "You yourselves have seen what I did to the Egyptians," God told them at Sinai, "and how I bore you on eagles' wings and brought you to myself" (Exod. 19:4). That image of the eagle will show up again as we look at Israel's second exodus, this time from Babylonian captivity, and discover what it means to God's people today.

Isaiah 40 introduces us to the Jewish exiles in Babylon whose faith in Jehovah God is about to be tested—for a faith that can't be tested can't be trusted. Even though the Jewish people hadn't always been obedient to His covenant, the Lord called them "My people" and claimed them for Himself. They had been living in Babylon for almost seven decades, but now Persia had conquered Babylon and Cyrus, king of Persia, was prompted by the Lord to release the exiles to rebuild their temple and their nation.

The massive grizzly, at first appearing threatening, becomes a pleasure to watch as it finds delight in shaking a snow-laden tree. Those things we fear are often no more than undiscovered blessings.

"Comfort, comfort my people, says your God" (Isa. 40:1). In this way the Lord addressed the Jewish nation and encouraged them to pack up and return home. "In the wilderness prepare the way of the LORD; make straight in the desert a highway for our God" (Isa. 40:3). It would take them over a month to go from Babylon to Jerusalem's ruins, and it wouldn't be an easy journey; but the Lord gave them the promises they needed in order to make the trip successfully. All they had to do was trust His promises and obey His statutes. Faith and obedience have always been the divine formula for God's people to do His will and achieve the impossible.

Israel had its beginning in the faith of Abraham and Sarah when they responded to God's call and had a personal exodus from Ur of the Chaldees. "By faith Abraham obeyed when he was called to go out to a place that he was to receive as an inheritance.... By faith Sarah herself received power to conceive, even when she was past the age, since she considered him faithful who had promised" (Heb. 11:8, 11). God promised this elderly childless couple they would not only bring many nations into the world, but that through one of them all nations of the world would be blessed.

Both promises came true. God gave them Isaac; later He gave Isaac and Rebecca twin boys, Jacob and Esau, and Jacob became the father of twelve sons, the founders of the twelve tribes of Israel. It was from the tribe of Judah that Jesus was born, and it is He who has blessed the whole world with the gift of salvation. From start to finish, it was an exercise of faith.

But what is faith, and why is it so difficult for people to believe? Faith is simply claiming God's promises and obeying what He says, in spite of the feelings within us, the circumstances around us or the consequences before us. Those three words—feelings, circumstances and consequences—explain why believing God can be so difficult. Each of them can be a source of fear, and fear and faith cannot live together in the same heart.

There is a response to overwhelming beauty that strikes the inner soul.

Humbled and broken we respond in reverence and awe to the Almighty Creator.

When the disciples thought they were drowning and they awakened Jesus to help them, Jesus asked them, "Why are you afraid, O you of little faith?" (Matt. 8:26). They were afraid because they looked at the circumstances around them—a terrible storm—and, concluding that death lay before them, gave in to their fears. "I have found a wonderful verse in my Bible," a woman told evangelist D. L. Moody, and she quoted Ps. 56:3—"What time I am afraid, I will trust in thee" (KJV). Moody replied, "I will give you an even better promise," and he quoted Isa. 12:2—"Behold, God is my salvation; I will trust and not be afraid" (KJV). Moody was right!

There is an unhealthy fear that *paralyzes* and a healthy fear that *energizes*, and we want to avoid the first and encourage the second. As we drive, we can ignore traffic signs and road conditions if we wish, but doing so is a mark of great folly, not great faith. In fact, it isn't faith at all; it's presumption. The little boy who imitated one of his comic book heroes and jumped out the window may have meant well, but he ended up in the hospital. Wise parents keep dangerous household items out of the reach of children and teach them early to obey stoplights, police officers and "No Trespassing" signs. A healthy fear of sickness, injury or death goes a long way to encourage sane living.

Knowing that the Jewish people would face difficulties and dangers on their journey from Babylon to Jerusalem, the Lord gave them a series of "fear not" promises to encourage them. He wanted them to travel by faith, not by sight, and to do that they needed promises. Their obedience was an act of faith based on promises from the Lord that could not fail.

But you, Israel, my servant…fear not, for I am with you; be not dismayed, for I am your God; I will strengthen you, I will help you, I will uphold you with my righteous right hand. (Isa. 41:8, 10)

For I, the LORD your God, hold your right hand; it is I who say to you, "Fear not, I am the one who helps you." (Isa. 41:13)

Fear not, you worm Jacob, you men of Israel! I am the one who helps you, declares the LORD; your Redeemer is the Holy One of Israel. (Isa. 41:14)

But now thus says the LORD, he who created you, O Jacob, he who formed you, O Israel: "Fear not, for I have redeemed you; I have called you by name, you are mine. When you pass through the waters, I will be with you; and through the rivers, they shall not overwhelm you; when you walk through fire you shall not be burned, and the flame shall not consume you. For I am the LORD your God, the Holy One of Israel, your Savior." (Isa. 43:1–3)

Fear not, for I am with you; I will bring your offspring from the east, and from the west I will gather you. I will say to the north, Give up, and to the south, Do not withhold; bring my sons from afar and my daughters from the end of the earth, everyone who is called by my name, whom I created for my glory, whom I formed and made. (Isa. 43:5–7)

But now hear, O Jacob my servant, Israel whom I have chosen! Thus says the LORD who made you, who formed you from the womb and will help you: Fear not, O Jacob my servant, Jeshurun whom I have chosen. For I will pour water on the thirsty land, and streams on the dry ground; I will pour my Spirit upon your offspring, and my blessing on your descendants. (Isa. 44:1–3)

Fear not, nor be afraid; have I not told you from of old and declared it? And you are my witnesses! Is there a God besides me? There is no Rock; I know not any. (Isa. 44:8)

In our Lord's parable of the talents (Matt. 25:14–30), the servant with one talent who failed his master and lost everything was the servant who was afraid. Instead of acting by faith and investing the money, he hid it and lost the opportunity to bless his master and win a reward for himself.

To be afraid of life, afraid of failing and afraid of trusting the Lord is to miss out on what God graciously offers us in this life. The Lord's "well done" is for servants who gladly accept the "little" and faithfully use it to produce "much" to the glory of God (Matt. 25:21). God's command to Joshua is His command to us today: "I will not leave you or forsake you. Be strong and courageous" (Josh. 1:5–6).

The Lord addressed His chosen people by two names: "Jacob" and "Israel." Jacob was his given name; it means "supplanter" or "one who trips others up and takes their place." But "Israel" means "he strives with God and prevails" or "a prince with God."

The Lord isn't ashamed to be known as "the God of Jacob," and that should encourage us. Like Jacob, we've done our share of scheming and trusting in our own ability to outwit others and get by. That God takes schemers and makes them into princes is pure grace. Because of the abundance of God's grace, we may "reign in life through the one man Jesus Christ" (Rom. 5:17). It's up to us whether we're going to have our own way and live like paupers or surrender by faith to God's way and live like kings, enjoying the riches of God's grace.

Our trust grows as we get to know people better, and our faith in God grows as we get to know Him better. We know God better as we read His Word, meditate on it and obey it: "But grow in the grace and knowledge of our Lord and Savior Jesus Christ" (2 Peter 3:18). It's possible to grow in Bible knowledge but not grow in grace, so that faith is in our head but not our heart. Bible knowledge itself doesn't change our character or conduct. "This 'knowledge' puffs up, but love builds up" (1 Cor. 8:1).

We also grow in our trust by experiencing the trials of life. According to Hebrews 11, the great men and women of Old Testament history glorified God and accomplished His will by trusting the Lord to help them overcome in difficulties. Nothing brings us to a loving trust in the Lord like going through the furnace of affliction with Him. "For the moment all discipline seems painful rather than pleasant, but later it yields the peaceful fruit of righteousness to those who have been trained by it" (Heb. 12:11). The fruitful life is the faithful life, not the comfortable life.

It is not pride but confidence portrayed
by the majestic eagle. It seems to have
understood the potential placed within
and has become certain of abilities
gained through trial and error, trial
and success.

The Jewish remnant trusted God's promises. They made their way successfully to their homeland, where they rebuilt the temple and re-established the nation. The times were difficult, but the people once again claimed the promises of God and trusted Him for the blessing they needed. "Not by might, nor by power, but by my Spirit, says the LORD of hosts" (Zech. 4:6). That same Holy Spirit is our Encourager and Enabler today. This brings us to the third stage in developing expert lifemanship—struggling.

Beware of despairing about yourself. You are commanded to put your trust in God, and not in yourself. – Augustine

Journeying across the broken terrain, we are suddenly faced with a seemingly insurmountable obstacle. It will take precious time to find a crossing point, but we are as certain of finding it as if a chart had been given.

3 Struggling

"The art of life," wrote British essayist William Hazlitt, "is to know how to enjoy a little and to endure much." His statement leans to the side of pessimism, or perhaps he considered it realism. But the Old Testament writers echo the human problem of suffering as well.

"Few and evil have been the days of the years of my life," said 130-year-old Jacob to Pharaoh (Gen. 47:9), and Job in his pain told his friends, "Man who is born of a woman is few of days and full of trouble" (Job 14:1). Moses wrote, "The years of our life are seventy, or even by reason of strength eighty; yet their span is but toil and trouble; they are soon gone, and we fly away" (Ps. 90:10).

As the Jewish exiles considered the long journey back to Israel after years in Babylon, most of the elderly must have felt powerless. You can't blame them; this march homeward wasn't exactly a victory parade. They were now free, but also much older than when they had arrived in Babylon, and the years had taken their toll. The people were going to a land ravaged by war and decayed by decades of neglect, and living there wouldn't be easy. Additionally, they would face the difficult tasks of restoring the nation and rebuilding Jerusalem and the temple.

Many of the exiles, young and old, chose to remain in Babylon, but about 50,000 Jews packed up and bravely journeyed to Judah. Some born during the Babylonian exile may have been eager to see this "land of milk and honey" they had heard so much about, and weren't deterred by the challenges of the journey. Youth is eager and the aged are cautious and prudent, but both are needed to accomplish God's work. The prophet Isaiah warned the young and the old that they needed each other; both groups needed the blessing of God in order to succeed. That lesson is essential today: Young people need the mature, and the mature need the young, and both need the Lord.

On this rugged coast wars have been fought and lives lost—but just now there is a peace as of the hand of God across the land. The cool updraft brings a healing mist, while flowers adorn the ruts formed by a struggle once deep and bitter.

"Even youths shall faint and be weary, and young men shall fall exhausted" (Isa. 40:30), warned the prophet, words that hardly painted an encouraging picture. Isaiah knew the road home would be a difficult one for the freed exiles, and the human body has its limits. It would be a struggle to walk the rough roads through deep valleys and over steep hills. If the young people couldn't make it, what hope was there for the older ones? Isaiah described the people as grass that withers, flowers that fade away and grasshoppers that last only a brief season (Isa. 40:6–8, 22).

On the road the people did become weary, and some may have fainted from exhaustion, but the faithful knew their weakness was God's opportunity to manifest His strength. "For when I am weak," wrote the apostle Paul, "then I am strong" (2 Cor. 12:10). In spite of their physical limitations, the citizens of Zion did make it home! "Some trust in chariots and some in horses, but we trust in the name of the LORD our God" (Ps. 20:7). God honored their faith, and He will honor our faith today.

There still remained an obstacle in their way, however—one more difficult to remove than the dangerous terrain. It was the obstacle in their hearts. Some of the people were holding a grudge against God; they didn't think He was doing enough for them. "Why do you say, O Jacob, and speak, O Israel, 'My way is hidden from the LORD, and my right is disregarded by my God'?" (Isa. 40:27). They were complaining that the Lord was ignoring their troubles, acting like an indifferent judge who refused to hear their case. "God doesn't care," was their attitude. "Doesn't He know what we're going through? Why doesn't He do something?" Isn't this the way we often think or speak when the going is tough?

But no matter how we feel about our circumstances, we know God cares because He has told us so! "What is man that you are mindful of him, and the son of man that you care for him?" (Ps. 8:4). "Casting all your anxieties on him, because he cares for you" (1 Pet. 5:7). How much more clearly could God express His concern for us?

But if God is so caring, why do people—even godly people—suffer? The noble attempts to answer that question have produced shelves of books and innumerable sermons, and we've yet to hear the last word on the subject. We know that we live in a fallen creation that is in "bondage to corruption" and is "groaning together in the pains of childbirth" (Rom. 8:21–22). We aren't

To know that changes and disturbances produce beautiful evenings is to welcome them. This calls to mind the words of a dear elderly friend who once said to me, "May you have just enough clouds in your life to make a beautiful sunset."

living in the Garden of Eden. We also know that we are born with a fallen nature, prone to resist God and to want our own way. Moreover, we have a strong enemy who takes advantage of our fallen nature to tempt us to oppose and disobey God. Life is a battleground, not a playground.

The day will come when God's people will see their scars become trophies for God's glory, but meanwhile, we have to fight the battles and feel the pain. One thing is for sure: When Jesus was born at Bethlehem, God Himself entered into the human arena and experienced all we do, and much more.

The greatest proof of God's love and the clearest answer to the question "Does God care?" is found at the cross. "God shows his love for us in that while we were still sinners, Christ died for us" (Rom. 5:8). Lay hold of this truth by faith and the question marks will eventually become exclamation points. You will find yourself praising the Lord instead of questioning Him.

Sometimes life is a struggle because we're out of God's will. That's why Israel was in Babylon. The nation had forsaken the true and living God and was worshiping the false gods of the pagan nations around them. The Lord sent them one prophet after another and disciplined them repeatedly to bring them to their senses. But they refused to submit, so He had to chasten them severely—He sent them to Babylon.

However, there are times when life is a struggle because we're *in* God's will and the enemy is opposing us. "Indeed, all who desire to live a godly life in Christ Jesus will be persecuted" (2 Tim. 3:12). The Lord puts us into difficult circumstances to help us mature in our faith and to prepare us for challenges He knows are coming. That's how He prepared Joseph, Moses, Joshua and David and an army of men and women who have served Him faithfully, from Bible times until today.

We don't really begin trusting God until we come to the end of ourselves and gladly yield to His gracious hand of discipline. "Weeping may tarry for the night," wrote King David, who had his share of suffering, "but joy comes with the morning" (Ps. 30:5).

But the point of the discussion is this: No matter how theologians and philosophers wrestle with the problem of evil, we have the privilege of living and we must make the most of it. Life comes at us like the traditional "speeding bullet," and we don't always have time to attend debates or listen to lectures before making life's important decisions. No matter what happens, life goes on—the life that includes the consequences of our decisions, good or bad, wise or foolish.

The American poet James Russell Lowell wrote, "There is no good in arguing with the inevitable. The only argument available with an east wind is to put on your overcoat." Jesus provides the "spiritual overcoat" we need. He said to His small group of disciples, "In the world you will have tribulation. But take heart; I have overcome the world" (John 16:33). "And this is the victory that has overcome the world—our faith" (1 John 5:4).

Living; believing; struggling. Unbelief is an invitation to be overcome, but faith gives us the opportunity to be overcomers, making the most out of life. If life's struggles make us stronger in faith, then they are working for us and not against us. By faith, we can learn to cooperate with the inevitable, which means turning our lives over to the Lord.

We could never learn to be brave and patient if there were only joy in the world. – Helen Keller

40

The fawn, only days old, instinctively finds a quiet, secluded resting place. Here it remains motionless, yet keenly aware of its surroundings. It will not stir unless prompted by its parent.

Waiting

The secret of expert lifemanship is not found in age or ability, for, Isaiah warned that even young men would grow weary and exhausted (Isa. 40:30). Nor is the secret in our circumstances, because these can be deceptive. In fact, the most difficult circumstances often teach us the best lessons and mature us the fastest.

A fundamental secret of expert lifemanship is *waiting.* "They who wait for the LORD shall renew their strength" (Isa. 40:31). This doesn't mean loitering and doing nothing, but tarrying with anticipation and faith, ready to do God's will.

On August 27, 1836, Ralph Waldo Emerson wrote in his journal, "There is a difference between the waiting of the prophet and the standing still of the fool." The "Sage of Concord" was right, and so was his friend Henry David Thoreau, who wrote, "All good abides with him who waiteth wisely." There's the key—waiting wisely and following the directions given by our Lord.

"Waiting wisely" involves four elements: entering God's presence, hearing God's voice, seeing God's glorious person and receiving God's strength. We do this by faith with the assistance of the Spirit of God, who teaches us the Word of God and helps us see the glory of God. His glory reveals His total adequacy for any challenges we face.

Waiting is not standing still; it's going forward in God's time and in God's strength. Expert lifemanship isn't cheap; there's a price to pay, and part of that price is waiting on the Lord.

ENTERING GOD'S PRESENCE

The titles of two books come to mind regarding this first aspect of waiting on the Lord. The first is *Hyperculture: The Human Cost of Speed* by Stephen Bertman. The second is *A Royal "Waste" of Time* by Marva J. Dawn. The theme of the first book is both obvious and ominous, but the theme of the second is not immediately apparent.

A Royal "Waste" of Time is about personal and corporate Christian worship, a practice that the world at large considers a waste of time. They might take a day off or even go on vacation, but that's not the same as bringing a quiet heart into the presence of God daily and setting our lives in order.

God gave His chosen people the Sabbath Day as a day of quiet rest, away from the demands of earning daily bread. But it wasn't simply a "day off," because it was "a Sabbath to the LORD" (Exod. 20:10). For us, the center of *each day* must be the Lord and His glory, not our own comfort and enjoyment. Yes, God "richly provides us with everything to enjoy" (1 Tim. 6:17) and He wants us to enjoy His gifts, but even more, He wants us to enjoy the Giver.

Our greatest need isn't entertainment; it's enrichment of the soul. That comes from taking time to get alone with God each day, to hear His Word and behold His glorious person—to receive the strength and wisdom we need to carry on for another day.

But waiting on the Lord isn't that easy. He's always available, but we're not always intentional. To rush into His presence, read a brief Bible passage or devotional thought, recite our routine prayers and hurry out into the "hyperculture" world is far from what God has in mind for us. His invitation to us is, "Be still, and know that I am God" (Ps. 46:10).

The words translated "be still" can also mean "take your hands off." It implies that we shouldn't try to micromanage our lives while God watches. "Delight yourself in the LORD, and he will give you the desires of your heart" (Ps. 37:4). Delighting in the Blessed One is far more important than delighting in His blessings. One is worship—the other could be idolatry.

"Be still before the LORD and wait patiently for him" (Ps. 37:7). God's book isn't a digest and His table isn't spread with fast food. If we're too busy to spend quality time with the Lord each day, then we're too busy, and it's time we got our priorities in order. This takes sacrifice and courage, because most of the people in our lives want us to stay in the fast lane and keep them company.

Henry David Thoreau said that he marched "to a different drummer," but too many people today are racing along to the rush of city traffic or the roar of a jet plane. They need to hear David say, "Wait for the LORD; be strong, and let your heart take courage; wait for the LORD!" (Ps. 27:14).

Waiting in the presence of the Lord requires sacrifice: We must give God time, one of the most precious commodities of life. Refusing to pay this price demands a greater and more painful price.

If we waste money, we can go to work and earn more; but if we waste time, we can't recover it. It's gone and so are the opportunities it offered us. When we devote time to the contemplation and worship of the Lord, it isn't wasted or lost; it's invested in the eternal and stays with us forever. As busy as He was, Jesus got up "early in the morning, while it was still dark … and went out to a desolate place, and there he prayed" (Mark 1:35). Jesus forfeited sleep that He might spend time with His Father and receive the strength He needed for that day.

My wife and I were once in a service where the worship pastor said, "For our closing hymn, we will sing number 325, 'Take Time to be Holy,' verses one and four." We didn't even take time to sing the entire song! After all, it was nearly noon and the restaurants would soon be packed.

44

But there's another factor involved in waiting before the Lord, and that's solitude. God's people need the encouragement of corporate public worship, but we can make no significant contribution to corporate worship if we're not practicing private worship.

Solitude isn't the same as loneliness, because you can be in the middle of a crowd and still feel very lonely. Psychologists write about alienation and estrangement, but neither one should be equated with solitude. Solitude is a choice, not a neurosis, and it's made by people who realize their busy public life must be balanced by quiet solitary time with God.

The Lord God said, "It is not good that the man should be alone" (Gen. 2:18), but that doesn't mean that everyone must be married or that all married couples must live in each other's hip pocket. Even people in love need private space and time in which to grow.

Solitary communion isn't solitary confinement. Solitude shouldn't be looked upon as restrictive, because it can bring wonderful freedom to us. People who feel trapped and afraid when alone probably don't know themselves, or if they do, they likely can't get along with themselves. They use people and activities as distractions to avoid facing themselves honestly—thus avoiding authenticity as a person.

It's essential that we get acquainted with ourselves, and solitude is one of the best ways to do it. Emerson wrote, "Nature delights to put us between extreme antagonisms.... Solitude is impracticable, and society fatal. We must keep our head in the one and our hands in the other. The conditions are met, if we keep our independence, yet do not lose our sympathy."[2]

In short, blessed are the balanced who can "go in and out and find pasture" (John 10:9). "I have learned in whatever situation I am to be content," the apostle Paul wrote from his prison cell (Phil. 4:11).

The word translated "content" means "self-sufficient, contained, independent of circumstances." How did Paul learn this valu-

The clear, cold air burns the skin. Movement or sound would betray the serenity of this peaceful daybreak. To wait in silence for the light's revelation of morning beauty is not an exercise in patience, but an expectation of grandeur to be displayed.

able lesson? He trusted God in his trials and worshiped Him in deliberate quiet times. The school of life and the school of prayer are still accepting willing students.

HEARING GOD'S WORD

When we come aside to worship and meditate, we can never be alone, for the Lord is with us and wants to speak to us from His Word. He longs to reveal Himself afresh to our eyes of faith and impart to us strength for the journey.

Jehovah wanted the Jewish exiles in Babylon to hear first of all a *word of comfort*.

> Comfort, comfort my people, says your God. Speak tenderly to Jerusalem, and cry to her that her warfare is ended, that her iniquity is pardoned, that she has received from the LORD's hand double for all her sins. (Isa. 40:1–2)

God could have opened this message with condemnation, but He began with comfort. The nation had sinned greatly and they and their descendants had suffered for it, but now the ordeal was over. God was speaking to them tenderly, "to the heart," calling them "my people" and affirming that He was their God.

They had every reason to be encouraged because they were no longer at war with God. He had pardoned their sins. They had been "paid in full" for their rebellion and now the Lord was dealing with them as a loving parent does after disciplining a child. "As one whom his mother comforts, so I will comfort you; you shall be comforted in Jerusalem" (Isa. 66:13).

The first thing we must do when we get alone with God is accept His gracious forgiveness and let Him affirm His loving relationship with us. The gift of life involves a series of new beginnings.

The profile of a healthy wolf reveals more than an effective hunter. Its keen ears are cupped toward its siblings, and it adjusts its concentration at the slightest variance in sound. How alert and sensitive and aware it appears.

After we have heard the word of God's comfort, we must then hear *His word of providence.*

A voice cries: "In the wilderness prepare the way of the LORD; make straight in the desert a highway for our God. Every valley shall be lifted up, and every mountain and hill be made low; the uneven ground shall become level, and the rough places a plain. And the glory of the LORD shall be revealed, and all flesh shall see it together, for the mouth of the LORD has spoken." (Isa. 40:3–5)

This passage is a description of an Eastern caravan: The ruler's servants were going before him to prepare the way as he and his entourage approached a city. It was important that they remove every obstacle and make the land as safe and level as possible for their master.

Through this picture, the Lord was telling His people that though the road seemed difficult and dangerous, He would journey with them and open their way. The Master would prepare the way for the servants! God's providence means that He plans ahead and is never taken by surprise—a ministry that makes possible the promise of Romans 8:28: "And we know that for those who love God all things work together for good, for those who are called according to his purpose."

As we pray about the day before us, we accept this promise by faith and we say with our Savior, "not my will, but yours, be done" (Luke 22:42). It's important that we not leave the place of prayer until we are surrendered to God's providential will, and happy with it.

Thirdly, we hear *God's word of assurance.*

A voice says, "Cry!" And I said, "What shall I cry?" All flesh is grass, and all its beauty is like the flower of the field. The grass withers, the flower fades when the breath of the LORD blows on it; surely the people are grass. The grass withers, the flower fades, but the word of our God will stand forever. (Isa. 40:6–8)

During the seventy years of captivity in Babylon, the Jewish people had seen two and probably three generations come and go, but God's promise never failed. He cared for them in that idolatrous land. He caused the Medes and Persians to defeat Babylon and then moved the new king, Cyrus, to proclaim freedom to the captives (2 Chron. 36:17–23).

The Lord has never broken His covenant with Abraham and his descendants and He never will. We change; circumstances and people around us change; but God's Word never changes, and "whoever does the will of God abides forever" (1 John 2:17). As we wait before the Lord and meditate on His Word, we receive assurance from Him and can face life with courage and confidence. "Heaven and earth will pass away," said Jesus, "but my words will not pass away" (Matt. 24:35).

SEEING GOD'S GLORY

The Lord ultimately revealed Himself to His people in all His beautiful character and majestic glory (Isa. 40:9–26). The Word of God reveals the God of the Word, as an old hymn expresses it:

> Beyond the sacred page
> I seek Thee, Lord;
> My spirit pants for Thee,
> O living Word.[3]

It isn't enough just to read the Word, think about it and perhaps even mark the statements that especially bless us. We must allow the Spirit to reveal the Lord to us in His Word.

Waiting on the Lord is a personal experience with God, and though we don't see Him with our human eyes, we do see Him with the eyes of faith. We need to have the eyes of our heart enlightened (Eph. 1:18) and pray with Moses, "Please show me your glory" (Exod. 33:18), which is another way of saying, "I want to know you better. Please reveal yourself to me." There are many people who know the history and theology of the Bible, but they don't know the Lord in a personal way. "That I may know him" (Phil. 3:10) was Paul's deepest desire, and it should be ours too.

Trekking through sand and clay is an arduous task. Distant rumblings bring an element of danger to the journey, adding to the struggle. But the apprehension caused by the approaching storm is greatly lessened by the beauty and power it displays.

The first revelation for the exiles was that of the Lord as *Conqueror.*

> Get you up to a high mountain, O Zion, herald of good news; lift up your voice with strength, O Jerusalem, herald of good news; lift it up, fear not; say to the cities of Judah, "Behold your God!" Behold, the Lord GOD comes with might, and his arm rules for him; behold, his reward is with him, and his recompense before him. (Isa. 40:9–10)

These are God's people Israel shouting the good news to the nations that their God—the God of Abraham, Isaac and Jacob—had redeemed them and was with them in their trials. He had permitted them to return to their land and rebuild Jerusalem and the temple.

There is no need for us to be afraid; the Lord will fight our battles and reward our work. He is the mighty Conqueror. As God's children, we don't fight *for* victory but *from* victory, the victory of Calvary's cross and the empty tomb. As we wait before the Lord, we can claim His victory, put on the armor by faith (Eph. 6:11) and go out to face the foe unafraid.

The second revelation of the Lord is that of the *loving Shepherd.*

> He will tend his flock like a shepherd; he will gather the lambs in his arms; he will carry them in his bosom, and gently lead those that are with young. (Isa. 40:11)

The mighty arm of the Warrior now becomes the tender arm of the Shepherd. Israel is "his people and the sheep of his pasture" (Ps. 100:3).

Jesus is our Shepherd today. He is the Good Shepherd who gave His life for the sheep (John 10: 11) and the Great Shepherd who equips His sheep and works in us (Heb. 13:20–21).

On those grand occasions that unexpected beauty envelopes a difficult day, the heart struggles for an appropriate response. We could weep for gladness or shout for praise—but silence seems most suitable, for

The picture here shows our Lord's concern for the next generation, for He carries the lambs and lovingly watches over the pregnant ewes. The future of all the nations rested with Israel, for "salvation is from the Jews" (John 4:22). As you wait before the Lord, you may feel as weak or helpless as a lamb among wolves, but there's no need to be afraid. The Shepherd's presence calms our fears (Ps. 23:4).

The third revelation depicts the powerful *Creator*.

Who has measured the waters in the hollow of his hand and marked off the heavens with a span, enclosed the dust of the earth in a measure and weighed the mountains in scales and the hills in a balance? Who has measured the Spirit of the LORD, or what man shows him his counsel? Whom did he consult, and who made him understand? Who taught him the path of justice, and taught him knowledge, and showed him the way of understanding?

Behold, the nations are like a drop from a bucket, and are accounted as the dust on the scales; behold, he takes up the coastlands like fine dust. Lebanon would not suffice for fuel, nor are its beasts enough for a burnt offering. All the nations are as nothing before him, they are accounted by him as less than nothing and emptiness. (Isa. 40:12–17)

God's "eternal power and divine nature," wrote Paul, "have been clearly perceived, ever since the creation of the world, in the things that have been made" (Rom. 1:20). Even without a Bible in our hand, we can look at the creation around us and know there is a God who has the wisdom to plan and the power to create and sustain this amazing universe. And this Creator is our Father because Jesus is our Savior! Neither nature nor nations can prevent Almighty God from accomplishing His purposes, because He is in total control. That ought to strengthen our faith!

The final revelation is that of the *true and living God.*

As I walk in the shadow of the Almighty, my eyes see a multitude of His principles illustrated in the things He has made.

To whom then will you liken God, or what likeness compare with him? An idol! A craftsman casts it, and a goldsmith overlays it with gold and casts for it silver chains. He who is too impoverished for an offering chooses wood that will not rot; he seeks out a skillful craftsman to set up an idol that will not move.

Do you not know? Do you not hear? Has it not been told you from the beginning? Have you not understood from the foundations of the earth? It is he who sits above the circle of the earth, and its inhabitants are like grasshoppers; who stretches out the heavens like a curtain, and spreads them like a tent to dwell in; who brings princes to nothing and makes the rulers of the earth as emptiness. Scarcely are they planted, scarcely sown, scarcely has their stem taken root in the earth, when he blows on them, and they wither, and the tempest carries them off like stubble.

To whom then will you compare me, that I should be like him? says the Holy One. Lift up your eyes on high and see: who created these? He who brings out their host by number, calling them all by name, by the greatness of his might, and because he is strong in power not one is missing. (Isa. 40:18–26)

Israel's besetting sin was worship of the false gods of the nations around them. They secretly practiced idolatry in Egypt, and they had no sooner received God's holy law at Sinai than they made a golden calf and held a sensual pagan feast. Once they were settled in the land of Canaan, they repeatedly abandoned the true and living God for the manufactured gods of the pagans around them, and the Lord had to discipline them over and over.

People today are tempted to trust in idols—money, achievement, possessions, other people—and leave the Lord out of their lives. In our waiting before the Lord each day, we must see His unequaled greatness and worship Him with all our heart, soul, mind and strength. To give lip service to the Lord while giving life service to false gods results in loss. It is to forfeit God's best gifts, invite His discipline and develop a kind of "religious schizophrenia" that divides our very being. Those who live this way are double-minded and unstable in all they do (James 1:8).

A bear cub must stay with its mother for its first eighteen months or face threats to its life from other animals, even other bears. At times the sow must leave her young alone in order to obtain food. During these moments the cub must not only wait quietly for her return, but must trust that she is nearby and will be there in an instant if needed.

Waiting before the Lord should integrate our lives, not divide them. Like the prophet Isaiah, we must see the Lord on His throne, "high and lifted up," and desire no other God but Him (Isa. 6:1–7). He calls each star by name, which is a staggering thought, and He knows us by name. How can we not worship and love Him?

RECEIVING GOD'S STRENGTH

Now we come to the conclusion of waiting on God.

> Have you not known? Have you not heard? The LORD is the everlasting God, the Creator of the ends of the earth. He does not faint or grow weary; his understanding is unsearchable. He gives power to the faint, and to him who has no might he increases strength. Even youths shall faint and be weary, and young men shall fall exhausted; but they who wait for the LORD shall renew their strength; they shall mount up with wings like eagles; they shall run and not be weary; they shall walk and not faint. (Isa. 40:28–31)

That's the true and living God. No wonder the psalmist ridiculed the gods of the pagans. "They have mouths, but do not speak; eyes, but do not see. They have ears, but do not hear; noses, but do not smell. They have hands, but do not feel; feet, but do not walk; and they do not make a sound in their throat" (Ps. 115:5–7). They can't help anybody, but they can cause terrible damage. "Those who make them become like them; so do all who trust in them" (Ps. 115:8). We become like the god we worship!

However, the God and Father of our Lord Jesus Christ made us in His image, and to become like Him is to have that image restored.

Consider this amazing statement: "And we all, with unveiled face, beholding the glory of the Lord, are being transformed into the same image from one degree of glory to another. For this comes from the Lord who is the Spirit" (2 Cor. 3:18).

Just as Moses came from the mountain with a shining face because he had waited in God's glorious presence (Exod. 34:29), so as we wait before the Lord we are transformed—transfigured—by the Spirit of God into the likeness of Jesus. The more we share His image, the more He shares His strength; and as we grow in His strength, we can increasingly fulfill our purpose in this world.

The word translated "renew" can also be translated "exchange": "But they who wait for the LORD shall *exchange* their strength . . ." (Isa. 40:31). Strength viewed as strength becomes weakness, but weakness viewed as weakness becomes strength. We exchange our strength for God's strength and find in Him the ability we need to soar like the eagle, to run without getting tired and to walk without giving up.

Let me put it this way. By waiting on the Lord and receiving His strength, we gain everything we need:

- the dynamic to do the impossible (soar like an eagle),
- the determination to accomplish the difficult (run without getting weary),
- and the discipline to maintain the routine (keep on walking without fainting).

Life is made up of the impossible, the difficult and the routine, and the Lord is adequate for all three challenges. In our human development, we first mastered the routine things—walking—and then tackled the difficult and the impossible—running and soaring.

But in the spiritual life, these are reversed. The most difficult thing in the Christian life isn't soaring like the eagle or running like the long-distance athlete, but walking day by day and successfully handling the ordinary demands of life without giving up.

In times of crisis, the Lord gives us wings and helps us fly. In times of heavy demands, He helps us run with patience so we reach the goal. But most failures don't come in the hour of crisis or the day of great demand, because in such times we know we can't make it without the Lord. Instead, we fail in the routine experiences of life when we feel confident we can handle the situation.

The scripture states that He "touches the mountains and they smoke." (Ps. 104:32).
One only needs to glance toward Him to see that He is there. How often my
yearning is only a response to His, that I would seek Him while He may be found.

Amazing and incredible are apt descriptions of the eagle's preparation for its nest. A secure location with a direct avenue of approach is chosen above the danger of intrusion. The area is purged of damaging matter and parasites, and up to a ton of material forms the foundation. The surrounding expanse beckons the nestling to fly from the convenience of its shelter.

Peter's great strength was his courage, and that's where he failed when he denied the Lord three times. Abraham's strong point was his faith, and he stumbled several times when he grew fearful or discouraged. David's strength was his integrity, but that's where he fell when he committed adultery, lied about it and covered his sin by murder. It was in the routine walk of life that they tripped and fell—and so will we if we get over-confident.

There are forces at work to pull us down, but God helps us fly higher. There are forces to hold us back, but God enables us to run farther. Forces attempt to tire us out, but the Lord helps us walk longer and not faint. This is expert lifemanship.

Patience is power. With time and patience the mulberry leaf becomes silk. – Chinese Proverb

On the coldest winter days, the eagle mounts up with joy, riding upon the currents at lofty heights. Its scream pierces the sky—a release of joyful passion in reaching an altitude at which it can soar.

5 Soaring

"They shall mount up with wings as eagles…"

We have considered three aspects of expert lifemanship—trusting, struggling and waiting—and now we shall look more closely at the blessings of soaring, running and walking that these disciplines bring to our lives. To the Jewish exiles in Babylon, soaring represented deliverance from bondage, running symbolized strength for the journey to their land and walking portrayed endurance to carry on the daily work of rebuilding the nation and the temple.

This work of restoration was the most demanding activity of all. Being set free from Babylon was an incredibly exciting experience and even the march to Judah had its joys as they contemplated living in their own land. But once they arrived in Judah, they faced one problem after another.

The Gentile nations around them interfered and tried to stop the work; they succeeded in delaying it for twenty years. The people didn't put the Lord first, so He couldn't fulfill His covenant and prosper their work. They built comfortable houses for themselves while neglecting to rebuild God's temple. The weather was bad and the harvests poor. The old men longed for "the good old days" of Solomon's temple. The younger Jews wished they were back in comfortable Babylon with friends and relatives who had stayed behind.

How does this apply to God's children today? Through faith in Christ, we have been delivered from the bondage of sin and we have lives to live, work to do and a God to glorify.

When harassed by ravens on a clear day, the eagle closes a hidden eyelid that allows it to fly directly toward the sun. The raven, not equipped with such provision, must drop away. Surely we must look toward the Son in similar times of attack.

- There are forces at work to pull us down and ruin us, but by waiting on the Lord, we can soar above circumstances and have the dynamic to do the impossible.

- There are forces to hold us back and make difficult demands upon us, but through Christ we can run the race and gain the determination to accomplish the difficult.

- There are forces attempting to wear us out, but by trusting the Lord, we can be disciplined to maintain an ordinary walk day after day, even when nothing exciting is on the horizon.

This is expert lifemanship.

If in New Testament days you had mentioned the eagle to a Jewish person, he would have scowled and perhaps spat in derision, since in those days the eagle symbolized the oppressive Roman government. But in Old Testament times the eagle was greatly admired. The Jews marveled at the eagle's swiftness of flight, its strength and endurance, its keen eyesight and its ability to soar in the heights for miles and miles.

Agur the wise man wrote, "Three things are too wonderful for me; four I do not understand," the first being "the way of an eagle in the sky" (Prov. 30:18–19). The Lord said to Job, "Is it at your command that the eagle mounts up and makes his nest on high?" (Job 39:27).

The important fact is this: God has created and saved us for the heights and we must learn to soar if we are going to please Him. We must trust the Lord for the dynamic to do the impossible. The pages of the Bible record impossible things God's people did when they learned to soar, as we'll see in the following extracts.

In Genesis 13, Abraham returned to Canaan from Egypt; it wasn't long before Lot's and Abraham's herdsmen started squabbling. God had given the land to Abraham, and he had every right to order Lot away, but he soared above the conflict and

The most difficult part of an eagle's "mounting up" occurs just after liftoff. There is a forceful pursuit of the higher places as gravity and crosswinds attempt to frustrate its efforts. Nevertheless, its eyes are fixed on the goal, and there is little faltering after its commitment is made.

gave Lot first choice of the land. No sooner had Lot claimed his land than the Lord appeared to Abraham and assured him that all of it belonged to him! Lot's selfish choice eventually led to the ruin of his entire family.

Abraham and Sarah had waited twenty-five years for their son Isaac to be born. In chapter 22, we read that when the boy was older, the Lord commanded Abraham to sacrifice him on an altar. To Abraham, this would cost more than the sacrifice of his only son whom he loved; it would also destroy his hope for the future. God had promised that Abraham's descendants would bring blessing to the whole world—but if Isaac died, there would be no descendants. Once again, by faith Abraham soared above the circumstances and obeyed the Lord, knowing that God always keeps His promises.

In chapter 37, Joseph's brothers hated him and schemed to sell him as a slave. He ended up in Egypt where the Lord was with him and blessed him, even in difficult circumstances. By the providence of God, Joseph became second in command over the land as well as the dispenser of food to people from famine-stricken lands, among them his brothers. On their arrival in Egypt, he recognized them, but they didn't know him. Joseph could have retaliated and had them punished, but instead he soared above their sins and the suffering they had caused him, and he chose to forgive them.

Through a series of carefully planned events, the Lord and Joseph brought the brothers to a place of repentance and then Joseph revealed himself to them, forgave them and was reconciled to them. He soared higher than they and brought heavenly grace down with him.

Exodus 19 records the Lord's meeting with Israel at Mount Sinai. There He reminded them of their miraculous deliverance from Egypt on the night of the exodus. "'You yourselves have seen what I did to the Egyptians,' said the Lord, 'and how I bore you on eagles' wings and brought you to myself'" (Exod. 19:4). Moses used that same image when he addressed the new generation at Canaan's entrance forty years later. "Like an eagle that stirs up its nest, that flutters over its young, spreading out its wings, catching them, bearing them on its pinions, the LORD alone guided him, no foreign god was with him" (Deut. 32:11–12).

The length and breadth of an eagle's powerful wings lead one to visualize its ability to lift its young to great heights. Though seldom observed, the basis for accomplishing such an act is obvious.

The Lord bore them from Egypt on eagles' wings and then guided and protected them as they traveled to the Promised Land. God wanted Israel to leave the nest and learn to fly, but, alas, they often wanted to return to Egypt and its security. Young eagles remain in the nest, high in mountain crags, for about one hundred days, and then the parent birds encourage them to leave and try their wings. If the eaglets flounder, the elder birds catch them, carry them and give them another chance. Eagles are made for the heights—and so are we. We may not like being coaxed out of the nest, but it's the only way to mature.

Exodus 32 tells of the difficult time Moses had leading Israel to their inheritance, not because of poor leadership, but because they were disobedient followers. The nation was made for the heights, but they insisted on going back to their sins and groveling in the depths. While Moses was communing with the Lord on Mount Sinai, the people made a golden calf and engaged in an idolatrous orgy. God declared He would blot out the people and from Moses make a new nation (Exod. 32:10). But Moses soared to the heights, interceding for Israel until God assured him He would protect the people and continue with them. God made the same offer to Moses when the people refused to enter the Promised Land (Num.14:11–19) and again Moses refused it. How tempting it would be for a great leader to build his own nation, but Moses resisted that temptation.

In the book of Ruth we read of a young widow from Moab, a nation rejected by the Lord, who had only her widowed mother-in-law to care for her. Ruth refused to stay in the place of her birth because she had trusted in the true and living God; she wanted to be with Naomi and God's other covenant people. Though widows were at the bottom of the social ladder in Israel, Ruth soared above her painful circumstances, humbly serving Naomi and trusting the Lord to help her. When she obediently put herself at the feet of Boaz, the lord of the harvest, things began to change; and the story ends with Ruth married to Boaz and giving birth to Obed, the grandfather of King David. If ever a woman mounted up with wings like eagles, it was Ruth.

The story of David and Goliath in First Samuel 17 is very familiar and illustrates what it means to mount up on the wings of faith. God gave David the dynamic to do the impossible and thereby bring great glory to the God of Israel. But David soared again and again in his career. In chapters 24 and 26, we are told that twice he had the opportunity to kill King Saul and both times refused to do so. Saul had mistreated David, lied about him and tried to kill him, but David wouldn't defile himself by

To be filled with potential like that of an eagle is humbling—yet we are invited to appropriate such a gift! As an eagle rises above the level of other fowl, it commonly expels a cry of victory that can be heard for miles around.

striking God's anointed. Instead, he used his eagle wings of faith, was lifted onto the currents of the Spirit and soared into the atmosphere of God's heavens.

In chapter 16 of the second book of Samuel, during the rebellion of Absalom, David was grossly slandered by Shimei. One of David's guards offered to kill the man, but David stopped him. "It may be that the LORD will look on the wrong done to me, and that the LORD will repay me with good for his cursing today" (2 Sam. 16:12). Jesus called this turning the other cheek (Matt. 5:39) and Paul said it was like putting coals of fire on somebody's head (Rom. 12:19–21). David knew not only how to rule his kingdom but also his temper. On that day, he soared above his enemies and grew in spiritual stature.

The background of Psalm 55 is probably the treachery of David's son Absalom in his attempt to dethrone his father and take over the kingdom (2 Sam. 14–18). David's dear friend and counselor Ahithophel joined with Absalom and this betrayal pained David very much. Jerusalem was filled with deception and danger and David had to flee to protect his life. He prayed, "Oh, that I had wings like a dove! I would fly away and be at rest; yes, I would wander far away…" (Ps. 55:6–7).

Anyone who has been in leadership knows to some degree what David was experiencing in those days. There are times when we grow weary of the burdens and battles and wish we could escape it all. But God wants us to be faithful to our calling and trust Him to see us through. We need to go into the holy of holies (Heb. 10:19–25) and commune with the Lord under the wings of the cherubim, for it's by waiting in His presence that we are strengthened for the responsibilities of life (Ps. 57:1).

David didn't need to fly away on the wings of a dove. He needed eagles' wings to lift him higher to fly above the circumstances. "In the LORD I take refuge; how can you say to my soul, 'Flee like a bird to your mountain…'?" (Ps. 11:1). We win the victory not by fleeing from the battlefield but by soaring above it, following the Lord of hosts.

Luke 23:34 tells us when Jesus was nailed to the cross, He prayed, "Father, forgive them, for they know not what they do." In Acts 7:60, Stephen prayed similarly as he was being stoned to death, "Lord, do not hold this sin against them." Jesus was impaled on a cross, yet He soared to the heavens, interceding for those who falsely condemned and illegally killed Him. Stephen was on his knees, feeling the painful impact of stones hurled by his enemies, yet he saw Jesus standing at God's right hand and soared like an eagle toward heaven. What a difference it makes when we ascend into heaven's atmosphere of grace and see God's perspective on our circumstances!

We are either overcome, or we are overcomers. "Do not be overcome by evil, but overcome evil with good" (Rom. 12:21). Our citizenship is in heaven (Phil. 3:20) and we seek to do the Father's will on earth just as it is done in heaven. "For everyone who has been born of God overcomes the world. And this is the victory that has overcome the world—our faith" (1 John 5:4).

The "earth dwellers," whose citizenship is only in this world (Rev. 11:10), live for worldly things and care nothing for the treasures of heaven. They are at home on earth; but believers are made for the heights. We have been raised to sit with Christ in heavenly places (Eph. 2:6) and we seek the things above (Col. 3:1–3). If our attention and affection are with Christ in heaven, then we are soaring, even though our bodies are on earth.

"But seek first the kingdom of God and his righteousness, and all these things will be added to you" (Matt. 6:33).

Aim at heaven and you get earth thrown in.
Aim at earth and you get neither. ~ C.S. Lewis

When called upon to run, the wolf maintains a steady gait in tireless pursuit of the goal. No matter how difficult the terrain or how great the challenge along the way, it does not deviate from it purposeful focus–for life will depend upon it.

6 Running

"They shall run and not be weary...."

When we wait upon the Lord, He will in His own time give us the dynamic to do the impossible—to "mount up with wings like eagles" and overcome in the crises of life. But we can't invest all our time soaring on heavenly currents, because here on earth there are tasks to be done and people to be served.

Setting our attention and affection on things above doesn't imply that we have no concern for circumstances and people around us. Evangelist D. L. Moody cautioned Christians not to be so "heavenly minded that they were no earthly good." Jesus went about doing good as well as preaching the good news of salvation, and He admonished us to let our lights shine by doing good works. "Do not neglect to do good and to share what you have, for such sacrifices are pleasing to God" (Heb. 13:16). We must have our feet on the ground while our minds and hearts are in the heavens.

We need the determination to do the difficult in spite of the forces that would hold us back: things like laziness, selfishness, sluggishness, procrastination, negligence, making excuses and getting discouraged. Each of us has a God-given vocation, and if we trust Him, He will provide what we need for accomplishing His will. Whatever our work may be, we want to do it faithfully for the glory of God. We can't be content simply to make a living; we need to make a life, and we want that life to glorify God.

76

If ever a person was a master of expert lifemanship, it was the apostle Paul. From the human point of view, he was a brilliant failure who threw away his career opportunities, devoting himself instead to Jesus Christ and to spreading the good news of His salvation. Paul was misunderstood and lied about; he was imprisoned and beaten; he went without food and sleep—and yet he never went without the joy of the Lord or the compelling desire to share Christ.

On Paul's return trip to Jerusalem after his third missionary journey, some of his friends predicted he would meet arrest and afflictions. Paul's reply was, "But I do not account my life of any value nor as precious to myself, if only I may finish my course and the ministry that I received from the Lord Jesus, to testify to the gospel of the grace of God" (Acts 20:24). My life—my course—my ministry. Keep these three priorities in place and you will "run and not be weary."

By using the phrase "my course," Paul was picturing life as a foot race, a metaphor used frequently by writers both ancient and modern. Foot races were important activities in both Greek and Roman athletics, and Paul was certainly acquainted with the races in the Olympian and Isthmian games. At the end of his life, as he waited for the Roman executioners, Paul wrote to his friend Timothy, "I have fought the good fight, I have finished the race, I have kept the faith" (2 Tim. 4:7).

To come to the end of your race having accomplished what God called you to do is the greatest achievement possible. That's the way Jesus felt as He faced the cross and looked back, for He said to the Father, "I glorified you on earth, having accomplished the work that you gave me to do" (John 17:4). May all of us be able to make that statement when we cross the finish line!

Jesus and Paul each saw their life's work as a divine stewardship; their responsibility was to accept their assignments gladly and faithfully complete them. In the Greek and Roman games, each runner was assigned a lane and was required to stay in it. That's what Paul meant by his "course." No matter what vocation God chose for us, if we're faithful to do it, then we are serving Him and are involved in divine ministry.

The busy mother who had on her kitchen wall a sign that read "DIVINE SERVICE IS CARRIED ON HERE DAILY" understood the meaning of her "vocation." One day we shall give an account to God and receive our reward, if we have been faithful. Salvation is a gift from God for all who trust Jesus as their Savior; but rewards will be given only to faithful believers who have fulfilled His will on this earth. "For we are his workmanship, created in Christ Jesus for good works, which God prepared beforehand, that we should walk in them" (Eph. 2:10).

It's unfortunate so many people view work as punishment which should by all means be avoided. They think the happiest people are those who have nothing to do, but quite the opposite is true. Idle people bore themselves and usually become difficult to live with and impossible to please. It's the people who do what God wants them to who find joy and satisfaction in life.

Work isn't punishment for sin, because Adam had work in the garden before sin appeared on the scene. "The LORD God took the man and put him in the garden of Eden to work it and keep it" (Gen. 2:15). Columnist and television personality Andrew Rooney wrote, "Working is so satisfying that if we didn't have to work, we'd have to invent some other reason for doing it."

How many retirees have gotten tired of idleness and gone to look for part-time jobs! They want to accomplish something and feel useful. Jesus saw work as nourishment, not punishment: "My food is to do the will of him who sent me and to accomplish his work" (John 4:34). Work isn't only making a living; it's making a life, fulfilling the purpose God has for us. It means becoming more and more like Jesus, the Master Craftsman. During the years before His public ministry, Jesus worked in Nazareth as a carpenter, building and mending things. Today we follow His example in the vocation God gives to each of us. Knowing this, we can "run and not be weary."

It's fascinating to discover the many athletic references in Paul's letters, for the Greek and Roman world of his day was caught up in sports just as our world is today. But there's this difference: The Greeks and Romans were *participants* in amateur athletics while the average sports fan today is a *spectator* at professional sporting events.

A beaver can fell a sapling in only minutes; much larger trees can be hewn as well, though it may take many hours of devoted labor. The beaver continues its efforts day and night, urged on by some joyful commitment to a greater work. It is most vulnerable while at this difficult task, yet the results are so important that it is rarely interrupted once it begins.

Spectators are good at cheering for the athletes; when the game is over, they go home shouting "We won!" You would think they had played on the team. Unfortunately, many Christian believers are better spectators than they are participants. They need to get out of the bleachers, join the team and be a part of the action.

Of course, this involves discipline and the expenditure of effort, and not everybody wants to pay that price. Paul wrote to Timothy, "Train yourself for godliness" (1 Tim. 4:7), and the word translated "train" gives us our English word "gymnasium." "Get into God's gymnasium," Paul is saying, "and let Him train you to become a winning Christian who can run and not be weary." The same word is used in Hebrews 5:14 and 12:11 reminding us of the work required to grow discipline and discernment.

Another New Testament word from the field of athletics is "agon"; it means "to struggle, to strive, to make every effort." (It is recognized in the English words "agony" and "agonize.") You don't become a winning long-distance runner by watching videos or listening to lectures. You have to eat properly, exercise regularly, make some personal sacrifices and get out there and run!

Remember, in the Christian race, we aren't competing against each other; we're competing with ourselves. We want to improve in every way and bring glory to the name of Christ. In the ancient games, the athletes who came in second or third went unnoticed; only the first place winner was rewarded. But in the Christian race, every contestant can receive a first place medal at God's throne. "Do you not know that in a race all the runners compete, but only one receives the prize? So run that you may obtain it" (1 Cor. 9:24). The second sentence is in the plural, which means that the prize is available to everybody in the church.

But our strength must come from the Lord. "For this I toil," wrote Paul, "struggling (agon) with all his energy that he powerfully works within me" (Col. 1:29). In Colossians 4:12 Paul applied the word agon to the prayer life of his friend Epaphras who was "always struggling on [their] behalf in his prayers." Epaphras put as much energy into his praying as the contestants put into their wrestling, running and boxing!

Against the wind and at temperatures of fifty below zero, the polar bear moves steadily toward its appointed destination. The bitter conditions freeze the pack ice, enabling the bear to reach the source of food vital to its survival. Nothing distracts it in the long struggle to be in the right place at the right time.

What would happen in churches today if everybody followed that example? Suppose Christian golfers got up to pray each morning as early as they got up to play golf? Suppose they put into their praying as much devotion and discipline as into perfecting their golf game? We could say the same about people who love baseball, football, swimming or any other legitimate sport. Prayer is a part of Christian warfare and it demands spiritual energy and serious motivation (Eph. 6:10–18).

Read one of Paul's classic passages on running the Christian race:

> Not that I have already obtained this or am already perfect, but I press on to make it my own, because Christ Jesus has made me his own. Brothers, I do not consider that I have made it [perfection] my own. But one thing I do: forgetting what lies behind and straining forward to what lies ahead, I press on toward the goal for the prize of the upward call of God in Christ Jesus. (Phil. 3:12–14)

"I haven't reached the goal yet," wrote the apostle, "but I keep it before me. I don't want anything to distract me lest I end up in the wrong lane and be disqualified. I'm not going to look back at my failures or even my successes. Instead, I'm going to look ahead and strive with all my God-given strength to reach His appointed goal for me. I'm straining every muscle and nerve—I'm bent forward and keeping my eyes on the goal. I haven't arrived yet, but by God's grace, I'll keep running and win the prize."

Paul had been a believer for at least thirty years when he wrote those words, yet he didn't feel like he had "arrived." That's a good attitude to have when training for God's Olympics.

From Paul's description of the Christian race, we discover that faith and endurance are the essentials for victory. A similar message is found in Hebrews.

The first light of morning reveals the summit, our intended destination. It is distant, yet appealing and distinct. As it beckons with revelations of its beauty, we joyfully advance—one step at a time.

Therefore, since we are surrounded by so great a cloud of witnesses, let us also lay aside every weight, and sin which clings so closely, and let us run with endurance the race that is set before us, looking to Jesus, the founder and perfecter of our faith, who for the joy that was set before him endured the cross, despising the shame, and is seated at the right hand of the throne of God. (Heb. 12:1–2)

It was after writing the great "faith chapter"—Hebrews 11—that the writer gave this admonition to endure in the race. The word "race" used here is again the word *agon*, and the words "endure" and "endurance" are key words in the Hebrew epistle (10:32, 36; 12:1, 2, 3, 7).

It is through "faith and patience" that we inherit God's promise to the winners (Heb. 6:12). The men and women of faith named in Hebrews 11 are not spectators, watching our race from heaven; they are winners in heaven who today bear witness to us in the Scriptures. They assure us the race can be won no matter who we are or what obstacles stand in the way. Their secret? Get rid of every hindrance and keep your eyes on Jesus, the greatest Victor of all. That is faith and endurance.

What excuses are we using to keep us from running our race this way? Whatever they are, there's somebody in Hebrews 11 who will refute them.

A retiree says, "I'm too old to start running the race." Abraham was seventy-five when he left his home and started for a land about which he knew nothing—and he didn't have a map. Moses was eighty when God sent him back to Egypt to rescue his people.

"But everybody's against what God wants me to do!" someone might say. The whole world was against Noah and no doubt laughed at him; but Noah turned out to be right.

"I've made so many stupid mistakes!" Then get acquainted with Jacob and be encouraged. God never abandoned him when

In holy silence before my Creator, I empty my burdened soul and am refilled with those things that are eternally vital.

he substituted scheming for believing and had to be disciplined, and Jacob ended his life triumphantly.

"Not many people are standing with me. We're outnumbered." Have you met Gideon? God trimmed his army from 32,000 men to 300—and they won the battle!

No, let's stop making excuses and fix our eyes of faith on Jesus Christ, the "founder and perfecter of our faith" (Heb. 12:2). We will never have to endure all that He endured on our behalf, and He can lead the way to victory. Jesus was at the starting line when we began the race, He's with us as we run and He'll welcome us at the finish line. So be encouraged! "And I am sure of this," wrote that great runner Paul, "that he who began a good work in you will bring it to completion at the day of Jesus Christ" (Phil. 1:6).

Like the Old Testament runners named in Hebrews 11, believers today must "also lay aside every weight, and sin which clings so closely . . ." (Heb. 12:1).

Note that little word "also." It tells us the Old Testament heroes of faith paid a price to enter and continue the race. Abraham was faltering in the race until he said goodbye to his father, brother and nephew Lot. Moses had to discover that it was God's hand and not his own that would deliver Israel; once he understood, He ran the race successfully. During the forty years between leaving Egypt and entering Canaan, Joshua had won many battles for the Lord, but they were now history. He had to meet Jesus at Jericho and surrender to Him, and Joshua recognized he was second in command (Josh. 5:13–15).

Depending on anything other than Jesus will trip us up; it has to be removed, even if it's a good thing. No sensible runner preparing for a race would deliberately gain extra weight and wear a loose-fitting robe and heavy boots on the track. If we want to win the prize, we have to pay the price.

On this and other occasions, I have observed a hurt or abandoned creature seek the solitude of a quiet and protected place. There it remains, still and silent until its strength returns.

When Jesus began His earthly race, He laid aside His heavenly glory and the independent exercise of His divine attributes, and came as a weak baby. Throughout the race, He obeyed the Father's will and glorified the Father's name. His race wasn't easy; He ran it just as you and I must run. Satan tempted Him to live by His own divine power, but Jesus chose to run by faith.

Jesus arose early in the morning and prayed. He trusted the promises of God's Word and depended on the power of the Holy Spirit. When He ended His earthly race, Jesus was hanging on a cross "despising the shame." His reputation was gone, His few possessions were gone and the disciples, except for John, were gone. The Father forsook Jesus when He became sin for us, and then His very life was gone.

The Good Shepherd willingly laid down His life for His sheep. He didn't shout, "I am finished!" but, "It is finished!" In spite of the devil's opposition, the failures of His disciples and the hatred of the religious leaders who didn't know God, He accomplished the work on earth God gave Him to do! He won the race that was set before Him—and He can help us win our race.

As we run, one of our greatest enemies is discouragement. The word "weary" in Isaiah 40:31 means much more than physical fatigue. It can also include disappointment, depression and that pessimistic "let down" feeling that blots out the sun and turns the future into a field of land mines. Our English word "discourage" literally means "without heart." When we're discouraged, we go through the necessary motions of life, but our heart isn't in it. Discouragement makes us want to drop out of the race completely.

In spite of Sir Winston Churchill's great leadership during the Second World War, he suffered painful periods of depression that he called his "black dog." Lord Beaverbrook said Churchill was either "at the top of the wheel of confidence or at the bottom of an intense depression." Yet it was Churchill who said, "There is one cardinal rule for the British nation—never despair." That's a great "cardinal rule," but how do you make it work? You wait upon the Lord.

To watch and listen is more than useless employment. Is it not a wonder that God's creatures endure the harshest weather and constant danger—and yet remain firmly committed to take a new stand day after day after day?

A discouraged person is a tired mind in a weary body surrounded with seemingly hopeless circumstances. The viruses of despair are always lurking in the neighborhood and they will read the signals, invade the system and change everything. Enthusiasm will become apathy, optimism will be replaced by melancholy, faith will diminish or vanish, self-pity will take over and the subject will see nothing but flickering lights on dead-end streets.

You lose your perspective and your priorities, and nothing anybody says or does seems to provide help. You try to pray and end up talking to yourself. You read the Bible but only see words and then quickly forget them. It's a terrible condition to be in, and the more you try to take control, the less adequate you feel.

Sometimes the most spiritual thing a person can do is rest. A perfect example is the prophet Elijah who got so depressed that he thought he was the only faithful believer left in the nation, and he wanted to die (1 Kings 18–19). On Mount Carmel, Elijah had led a great victory against idolatry as he called down fire down heaven and prayed up a storm that ended a three-and-a-half year drought. Then Queen Jezebel threatened to kill him.

Elijah didn't realize what all these intense experiences were doing to his physical and emotional circuitry, and sure enough, he became fearful and depressed and ran off to hide. So the Lord told him to take a nap. God sent an angel to bake him a cake, and the combination of food and rest gave him what he needed to finish his journey.

If you go without food and rest, and brag that you're "trusting the Lord," be careful you aren't tempting the Lord. We think we're made of steel, but God knows we're made of dust. Sometimes we must learn that lesson the hard way. Even Jesus admonished His disciples to take time to rest after they had returned from a difficult ministry trip (Mark 6:30–32). Vance Havner used to say, "Either we come apart and rest, or we come apart."

We expect to get tired as we do good—even Jesus needed to rest (John 4:6)—but we don't want to get weary of doing good (Gal. 6:9). To be tired in the Lord's work is one thing; to be tired of the Lord's work is quite something else.

There came a time in the life of Jeremiah the prophet when he was perplexed and weary (Jer. 12:1—4). God's reply to his questions needs to be heard today: "If you have raced with men on foot, and they have wearied you, how will you compete with horses? And if in a safe land you are so trusting, what will you do in the thicket of the Jordan?" (Jer. 12:5).

Running the race isn't easy, and it doesn't get easier. It's a basic principle that easier human skills are developed early in life; then, as we mature, we start to grapple with harder challenges. Meeting each challenge successfully prepares us for meeting the next one.

The world's greatest pianist started by locating middle C and learning the scales, and the greatest author began by learning the alphabet and how to spell. Jeremiah had raced with people but now he had to race with horses. His faith was strong in his hometown of Anathoth, but how confident would he be in the thick jungle near the Jordan River? The Babylonian army was going to invade the land and destroy Jerusalem! Could Jeremiah handle the challenge?

Can we handle the challenge? Yes, we can, if we focus our eyes of faith on Jesus and trust Him as He trusted His Father. To watch the other runners will distract us and perhaps discourage us. We must run in our own lane and at our own pace, and remember that we're competing with ourselves and not anyone else. We must not be surprised as the challenges become more difficult nor should we depend on our own experience or ability. Solomon was right: "The race is not to the swift" (Eccles. 9:11). God still chooses "what is weak in the world to shame the strong ... so that no human being might boast in the presence of God" (1 Cor. 1:27, 29). There is nothing God cannot do for those who want Him to have the glory.

Don't bother to give God instructions. Just report for duty. ~ Corrie ten Boom

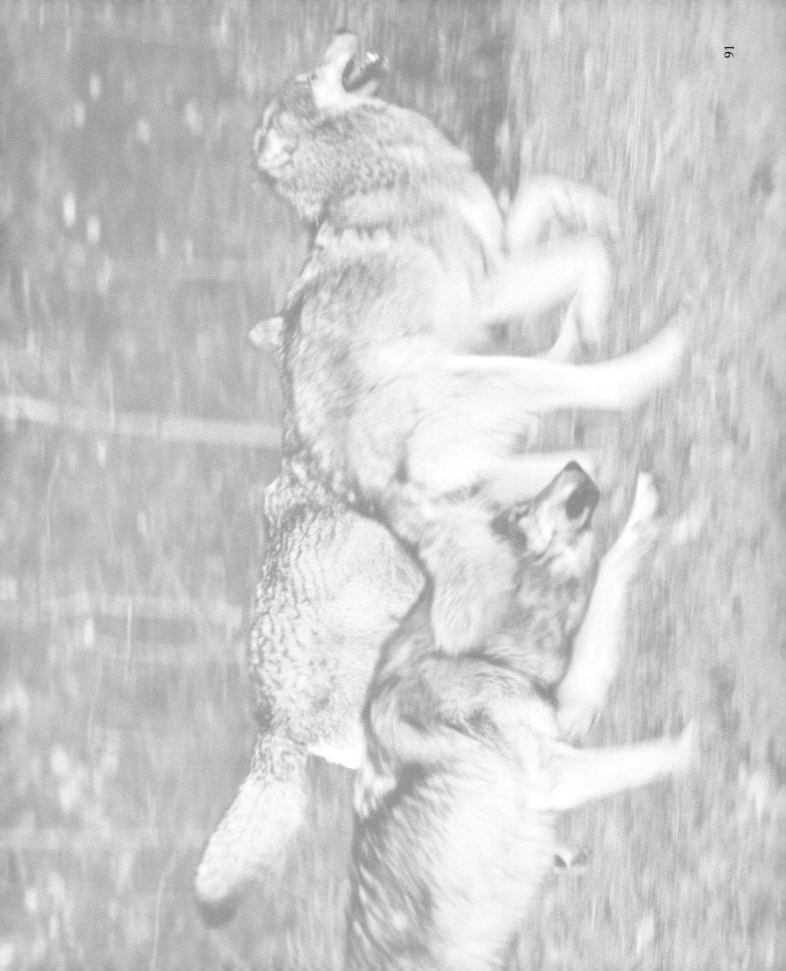

Much to my amazement, I have often observed the eagle walking where I would expect it to be flying. Perhaps it has come to cleanse its feathers after a rain. But walking in the beauty of its surroundings, it is perfectly content to be grounded in such a delightful place.

Walking

"They shall walk and not faint."

The man that historians call "the father of modern missions" was a humble English cobbler named William Carey (1761–1834). He had a burden to take the Gospel to other nations. As he made and repaired shoes, he taught himself Hebrew, Latin, Greek, French and Dutch. Then Carey became a pastor and urged the neighboring pastors to start emphasizing foreign missions. In 1792 he helped to organize a missionary society and the next year went to India as a missionary. In spite of numerous difficulties, he and his associates had a remarkable ministry there, not only in evangelism but also in the areas of Bible translation, publishing and education.

In his latter years, when Carey was asked about someone writing his biography, Carey replied: "If he gives me credit for being a plodder, he will describe me justly. Anything beyond this will be too much. I can plod. I can persevere in any definite pursuit. To this I owe everything."

Plodding. Persevering. Walking and not fainting. Samuel Johnson wrote, "Great works are performed not by strength but by perseverance." One wit said the mighty oak was only a little nut that stuck to the job, and another said we should imitate the postage stamp because it stuck to one thing until it got to its destination. In expert lifemanship, there's a time for soaring and for running, but more often our work is accomplished by plodding, a step at a time, a day at a time.

Our progress isn't always steady or easy, and we often encounter disappointments, but we keep on going. Charles Spurgeon said, "By perseverance, the snail reached the ark." When he was president of Wheaton College, Dr. V. Raymond Edman often reminded the students, "It's always too soon to quit." In the fable of the turtle and the hare, the hare had all the advantages, but the turtle knew how to persevere and he won the race.

There's nothing spectacular about walking. It's an ordinary activity performed daily by billions of ordinary people as they carry on an infinite number of ordinary tasks. If all of us wore pedometers, we'd be amazed how many miles we walk during an average week. Yes, there are many people who drive their cars three blocks to the health club so they can exercise. However, more and more people are discovering the delightful health-giving benefits of old-fashioned walks.

We've already learned that running is a biblical metaphor for doing our God-given work and reaching our God-appointed goal. Walking is a metaphor for our fellowship with the Lord each day and is an important part of building character and becoming like Christ.

Before they disobeyed God, Adam and Eve walked with the Lord in their garden home (Gen. 3:8). Enoch walked with God and escaped the flood when he was carried alive to heaven (Gen. 5:22–24). Noah walked with God and was taken safely through the flood (Gen. 6:9), and Abraham walked with the Lord and enjoyed His fellowship for a century. The Lord not only dwelt in the tabernacle in the center of Israel's camp, but He graciously walked among the people and claimed them as His own (Lev. 26:12).

God wants to fellowship with His people and we should desire fellowship with Him. God is seeking people not only to worship Him (John 4:23) but to walk with Him and enjoy His companionship. If we walk with Him in faith and obedience, His promise is "and I will be a father to you, and you shall be sons and daughters to me, says the Lord Almighty" (2 Cor. 6:18).

It's becoming more and more difficult to find shoe repair shops, and there are at least two reasons. For one thing, we live in a throwaway society, and as fashions change we dispose of the old and purchase the new. Depending on the shoe style, new soles and heels may cost nearly as much today as a new pair of shoes, because many shoes are manufactured to be disposable. The styles of shoes advertisers encourage children and teens to buy are very expensive and can't be repaired. Economists call this "built-in obsolescence."

But the second cause may be that people don't walk as much as did previous generations, so they aren't wearing out their shoes. I grew up during the Depression, and many times I had to deliver worn family shoes to Mr. Criswell's shoe repair shop and pick them up when they were repaired. We weren't ashamed to wear mended shoes any more than we were ashamed to wear mended clothing. But few people these days walk enough to wear out their shoes. Until they turn sixteen and have a driver's license and a car, the average teenager expects mom and dad or the school system to provide transportation, or they ride with older friends. Most children and adolescents don't want to be seen walking anywhere. Their social standing might suffer.

Accustomed as we are to instant information, fast food, the internet and MTV, today's society is in a terrible hurry and is paying a great price both physically and emotionally. Pascal wrote, "I have discovered that all the unhappiness of men arises from one single fact, that they cannot stay quietly in their own chamber." He lived from 1623 to 1662, and if he thought people were nervous and overly stimulated in his day, he should see what's going on today!

I have watched and pitied people I've seen rushing through airports with a cell phone in one hand, a palm pilot in the other and a bulging flight bag hanging from their shoulder. They are desperately trying to save a few minutes so they can grab a sandwich. I've also watched them on the plane, exhausted and staring into space, wondering if they dare take a nap when there's so much work to do before they get to their next appointment.

It surprises people to discover God isn't in a hurry. He waited twenty-five years before he gave Abraham and Sarah their son Isaac. He spent thirty years preparing Joseph to be the second in command of Egypt. He waited eighty years before He called Moses to deliver the Israelites from Egypt, and thirty years before putting David on the throne of Judah. Even Jesus waited

Deliberate in their journey's direction, the grizzlies walk steadily for hours until they pass out of sight in the distant valley. With only an occasional pause to survey the land before them, they move untiringly ahead. What prompts this determination through such difficult terrain?

in His public ministry.

...ader and you will see the importance of waiting and preparation. But history isn't the witness of nature tells the same story. God could unveil spring overnight, but ...adually. He could produce the harvest in a few days, but He takes a summer season ...b for nine months before it's born because that's the way God planned it. God can ...rs for Him to grow stately oaks.

...ufactured while you wait," but then I realized it summarized the basic philosophy of ... preparing and maturing. Why should leaders waste time learning the ropes when a ...eans of instant success?

...e piano, teach school or drive a car, one of the best ways to learn is to watch an ex-...s and learn the basics, but we also learn by paying attention to good examples. Mark ...t up with than the annoyance of a good example," but that's how he learned to pilot

...v good examples, and some of the best are found in the Bible. Some show us what not ...sus is the perfect example. You will meet many people as you read your Bible, and they ...2:6 sums it up best: "Whoever says he abides in [Jesus] ought to walk in the same way ..."so that you might follow in his steps" (1 Pet. 2:21). He is the best example of all.

...meditate upon the life of Jesus Christ," wrote Thomas à Kempis on the first page of his *Christ*, first published in 1470. It has been in print ever since. I recommend it to you.

The mother bear knows the thickness of the ice and the location of danger. She will guide her young, providing nourishment and protection when necessary. Her example will allow them to survive as they recall and repeat her behavior.

The entire Bible is important to us; but if you want to have a transforming experience, devote some time to reading Matthew, Mark, Luke and John over and over again. Use different translations if you wish, but concentrate on these books and the example of Jesus Christ revealed in them.

What was His manner of life? What were His priorities? How did He treat His enemies? How did He instruct His followers? Was He ever angry or disappointed? What kind of prayer life did He have? How did He use the Scriptures? What made Him joyful? What grieved Him? How did He handle interruptions? How did He face danger and death?

As you read and meditate, seek to discover the eternal principles that are applicable to your life today. By following the example of Jesus, we can experience the grace and guidance we need in our complicated world. Our Lord's example points the way, and the Spirit of God enables us to follow and "walk in the same way in which he walked" (1 John 2:6).

The Bible tells us what kind of "walk" we should have in this present evil world. The Lord insists we be different from the crowd around us and walk "in newness of life" (Rom. 6:4). Why? "The old has passed away; behold, the new has come" (2 Cor. 5:17).

This means that we "walk in a manner worthy of God" (1 Thess. 2:12) because we are God's children through faith in Christ. We "walk in love, as Christ loved us" (Eph. 5:2), and we walk "as children of light" because "God is light" (Eph. 5:8, 1 John 1:5). "Look carefully then how you walk" (Eph. 5:15), which means we exercise wisdom and don't waste our God-given opportunities. "Therefore do not be foolish, but understand what the will of the Lord is" (Eph. 5:17). God has prepared the good works He wants us to accomplish and "we should walk in them" (Eph. 2:10).

We must remember that our Lord walks with us, for He has promised never to forsake us (Heb. 13:5). Following Jesus, we go "from strength to strength" (Ps. 84:7) and from grace to grace (John 1:16), and He is adequate to meet every need.

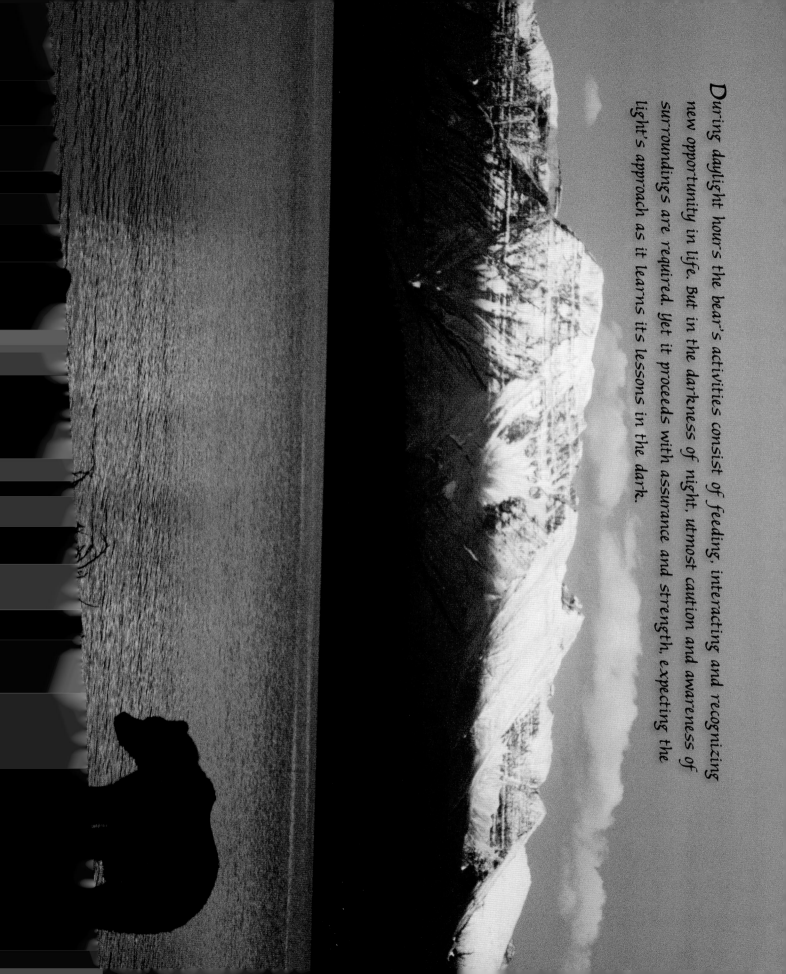

During daylight hours the bear's activities consist of feeding, interacting and recognizing new opportunity in life. But in the darkness of night, utmost caution and awareness of surroundings are required. Yet it proceeds with assurance and strength, expecting the light's approach as it learns its lessons in the dark.

I think it's important that we begin each day by meeting with the Lord and investing quality time reading the Word and praying. Communion with God isn't an accident; it's a holy appointment. "Do two walk together, unless they have agreed to meet?" (Amos 3:3). If we want God to walk with us all day, we had better meet Him before the day becomes cluttered, checking with our Master for the day's orders. We must keep in mind that He is our Commander. The discipline of a morning meeting with the Lord is one of the secrets of expert lifemanship.

"Beaten paths are for beaten men," said Eric A. Johnston, American business leader and motion picture executive. If he means that we need more far-sighted pioneers who will cut new paths in some areas of life, then this statement is true. But when it comes to building character and strengthening personal relationships, Mr. Johnston is wrong. The old paths are what we need.

The public thrives on novelty, and like the Athenians in Paul's day, people "spend their time in nothing except telling or hearing something new" (Acts 17:21). Expert lifemanship is built on timeless truths that work in any age. At the close of a full and successful life, David wrote, "He leads me in paths of righteousness for his name's sake" (Ps. 23:3), and the word translated "paths" means "deep ruts, the beaten paths that others have walked."

For every new book I read, I probably re-read two or three older books. Like Isaac, I dig again the old wells (Gen. 26:18); like David, I walk in "the beaten paths"; and like Jeremiah, I ask for "the ancient paths" marked out by God (Jer. 6:16). The quest for novelty leads to a shallow life; the appreciation of the "beaten paths" helps us to develop moral and spiritual depth. We don't "live in the past" as though life was a museum, but the past lives *in* us; without it we would lose our way.

Enoch walked with God. One day, unexpectedly, his earthly walk was ended by his call to heaven. Enoch and Elijah are two believers who didn't walk through the valley of the shadow of death but were taken bodily to heaven. If Jesus were to return today, the millions of believers on this earth would have the same experience and be caught up "in the clouds to meet the Lord in the air, and so we will always be with the Lord" (1 Thess. 4:17).

It is rare when journeying a lengthy road to see hope's reward in the distance. Blessed are those who have yet to see, but maintain their hope on the pilgrimage to our eternal home.

Will our walk with the Lord end? By no means! Jesus promises that believers who keep themselves undefiled in this present evil world will walk with Him in white and be honored at the throne of God (Rev. 3:4–5). Our walk on earth determines our welcome in heaven. Faithful believers will "receive a rich welcome into the eternal kingdom of our Lord and Savior Jesus Christ" (2 Pet. 1:11, TNIV), and the Lamb will lead them to "springs of living water" (Rev. 7:17). Unfaithful believers "will be saved, but only as through fire" (1 Cor. 3:15).

We must be alert and keep our garments unspotted, because we don't know when our Lord will return. "Surely I am coming soon" (Rev. 22:20). Then, like Enoch, our earthly walk will end and we will walk with Jesus, clothed in white!

We are always sowing our future; we are always reaping our past. – William Ralph Inge, Dean of St. Paul's, London

In the wanderings of a sensitive individual, a setting is at times discovered which words cannot describe. To intrude would be irreverent. The heart bows in gratitude for the exceeding abundance beyond all we could ask or imagine.

Abounding

"I came that they may have life and have it abundantly." (John 10:10)

Two stories come to mind.

The first is about a New York City street urchin who was struck by a car and taken to the hospital. When he was in bed after being treated, a nurse brought him a large glass of milk, and he just stared at it. "Is something wrong?" she inquired. He looked at her and asked, "Do I get all of it?"

The second is about a poor mountain woman who made a once-in-a-lifetime trip to the North Carolina coast to visit her sister. As she stood on the shore, staring at the Atlantic Ocean, she began to weep. "Why are you crying?" her sister asked, and she replied, "It's just wonderful to see something that there's plenty of!"

Those who practice expert lifemanship are not automatically protected from pain or tears or the many common burdens of life. In fact, it sometimes seems they have more than their share of difficulties. But because they have life in Christ, they can overcome. They will soar in a looming crisis; in times of challenge, they will run and not get weary; and in the daily routine they will continue walking—plodding, if you please—without feeling faint. This is the "abundant life" Jesus came to give—not the absence of difficulties but the ability to transform them into joyful victories to the glory of God.

Paul called it being "more than conquerors through him who loved us" (Rom. 8:37). John spoke of "the victory that has overcome the world" (1 John 5:4). David described it vividly, "My cup overflows" (Ps. 23:5). Expert lifemanship means living by the overflow, not the undertow. It means trusting our heavenly Father to keep His promise: "And my God will supply every need of yours according to his riches in glory in Christ Jesus" (Phil. 4:19). His provision is the secret of our peace.

The Scottish preacher George H. Morrison defined peace as "the possession of adequate resources." Some, though, live out the reverse of this statement, "the resources of adequate possessions." Jesus warned that "one's life does not consist in the abundance of his possessions" (Luke 12:15). Yes, our Father knows that we need the basics of life (Matt. 6:32), but we need to remember that there's a difference between our need and our greed, or what Mark Twain called "the unnecessary necessities."

In today's "success society," advertisers create appetites in consumers so they will become customers. They encourage people to spend money they don't have for products they don't need so they can "keep up appearances" which really don't matter. Thoreau was correct when he wrote, "A man is rich in proportion to the number of things he can afford to let alone." Expert lifemanship follows the philosophy of Jesus and the apostle Paul—"as poor, yet making many rich" (2 Cor. 6:10).

Our Father is a God of abundance. He longs to share His bounty with His children when they have need. He said to Moses: "The LORD, the LORD, a God merciful and gracious, slow to anger, and abounding in steadfast love and faithfulness, keeping steadfast love for thousands, forgiving iniquity and transgression and sin..." (Exod. 34:6-7).

This is true theology and a recurring theme in the Old Testament. "But you are a God ready to forgive, gracious and merciful, slow to anger and abounding in steadfast love..." (Neh. 9:17). "But you, O Lord, are a God merciful and gracious, slow to anger and abounding in steadfast love and faithfulness" (Ps. 86:15).

Because our God has these wonderful attributes, it's our responsibility to worship Him and do His will. "Return to the LORD your God," implored the prophet Joel, "for he is gracious and merciful, slow to anger, and abounding in steadfast love..." (Joel 2:13).

It isn't enough to *know* about God's character; we must *respond* to Him with obedience and love. The prophet Jonah could mouth correct theology, but he failed to obey the Lord from his heart (Jonah 4).

Life today is so complicated with millions of people depending on electronic devices to get them through the day. Most can't drive down the street and quietly meditate; they need a cell phone in one hand and a cup of coffee in the other. They work hard eight hours a day, five days a week, to be promoted to work twelve hours a day, seven days a week—and be away from home most of that time. They have all the "things" money can buy but can't enjoy them, having gradually lost the things money can't buy.

They need to simplify their lives, focus on values instead of prices and on pleasing God instead of people. If they learned to live a day at a time, they would discover what David meant when he wrote, "My cup overflows" (Ps. 23:5). He wasn't speaking about dividends on his financial investments but on his spiritual ones. Psalm 23 opens with, "The LORD is my shepherd; I shall not want." When you submit to Christ as your Shepherd—your only Shepherd—and follow Him, He begins to change your life and lead you step by step into expert lifemanship.

One of the first changes is that we will begin living *one day at a time*. This doesn't mean we don't make plans for the future, but that we stamp each plan with IF THE LORD WILLS (James 4:13–17). God arranged our universe so everything operates on a twenty-four-hour cycle of day and night. All nature follows this schedule. Thanks to modern technology, we can travel from night to day or even stay home and turn night into day. But too much of this puts us out of sync with the scheme of things and will involve a costly price.

It's been rightly said that many people in western society today are being crucified between two thieves—the regrets of yesterday and the fears of tomorrow—so they don't have time and energy to enjoy today. Unfortunately, this western malady has been exported eastward and people who were once calm and meditative have become nervous and competitive. God's promise to His children is "as your days, so shall your strength be" (Deut. 33:25). There is always time for the will of God, and He

The elements of a lovely scene are often a reflection of a lovely life with the Savior. There is a constantly flowing stream, an abundance of colorful offerings, a rock solid foundation—and the encouragement of Light to illuminate it all.

always provides the strength we need to do it. "The eternal God is your dwelling place, and underneath are the everlasting arms" (Deut. 33:27).

Living a day at a time means depending on God's faithfulness daily. "The steadfast love of the LORD never ceases; his mercies never come to an end; they are new every morning; great is your faithfulness" (Lam. 3:22–23).

Jeremiah wrote those words at Israel's lowest point in history. They had rebelled against God and broken the covenant; God's longsuffering had run out and He had to discipline them. The Babylonian army came and devastated the land, destroyed Jerusalem and the temple, and took thousands of Jews captive to Babylon. Instead of looking back and wishing for a world that could never be, Jeremiah accepted each new day as a gift from the Lord, an opportunity for a new beginning. Jeremiah could depend on God's care—"Give us each day our daily bread" (Luke 11:3)—and so may we.

Every day we must hear God's voice through His Word, because that Word is our daily strength and wisdom. "And day by day ... he read from the Book of the Law of God" (Neh. 8:18). Jesus quoted Moses (Deut. 8:3) when He said, "Man shall not live by bread alone, but by every word that comes from the mouth of God" (Matt. 4:4).

Jesus began each day meditating on the Scriptures and hearing His Father's voice. "Morning by morning he awakens; he awakens my ear to hear as those who are taught" (Isa. 50:4). "I do nothing on my own authority," said Jesus, "but speak just as the Father taught me" (John 8:28). If the holy Son of God had to depend on a daily word from the Father, how much more do we need to hear!

We must not keep the Word to ourselves but share it with others. "The Lord GOD has given me the tongue of those who are taught, that I may know how to sustain with a word him who is weary" (Isa. 50:4). How many weary people in our world need to hear from us a sustaining word from God!

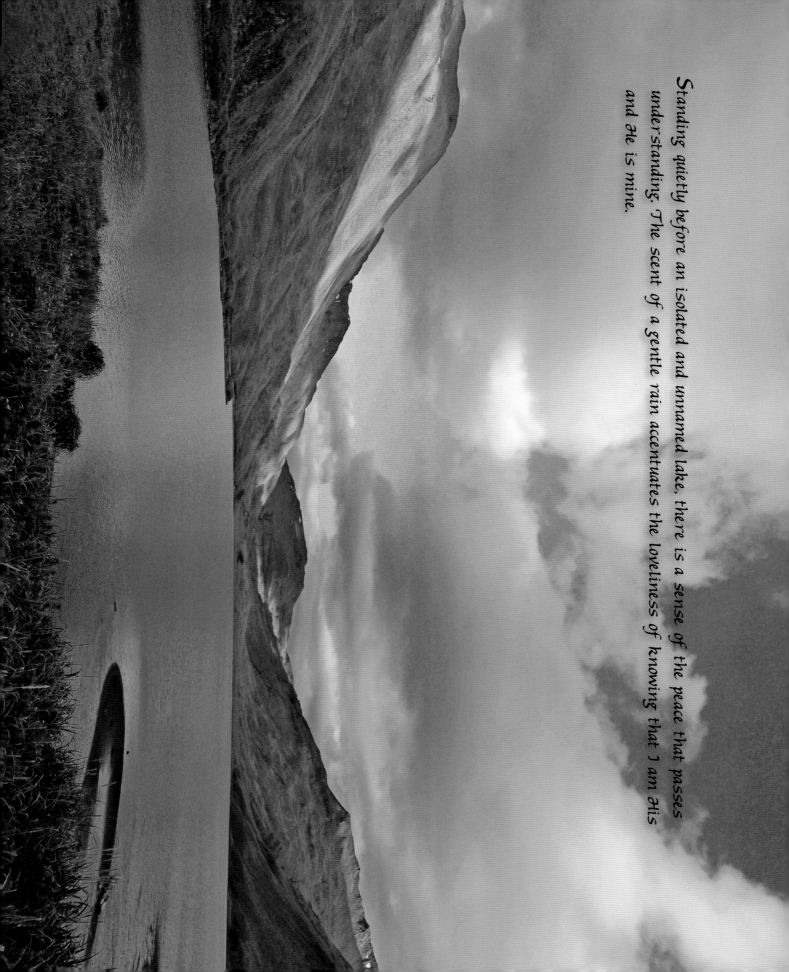

Standing quietly before an isolated and unnamed lake, there is a sense of the peace that passes understanding. The scent of a gentle rain accentuates the loveliness of knowing that I am His and He is mine.

Living a day at a time means praising the Lord every day, no matter what the burdens or circumstances may be. We must be like the priests and Levites in the days of King Hezekiah who "praised the Lord day by day, singing with all their might to the Lord" (2 Chron. 30:21). Complaining only makes our situation worse and lets others know we don't really believe God knows what He's doing.

It's much easier to face difficulties when we sing to the Lord than when we argue with Him. Our praise may not alter the circumstances around us, but it will certainly change the landscape within. Jesus sang a hymn before He went out to die on the cross (Mark 14:26). Surely we can sing praise to God as we face the difficulties of life.

If we're faithful to live a day at a time, another blessing will come to us: We will become more and more like Jesus Christ. "So we do not lose heart. Though our outer self is wasting away, our inner self is being renewed day by day. For this light momentary affliction is preparing for us an eternal weight of glory beyond all comparison" (2 Cor. 4:16–17). The afflictions of life aren't working against us but for us, and are making us more like the Savior. And the more we become like the Lord Jesus, the more we will experience expert lifemanship day by day.

Not only is He the Example, but He is also the Enabler for following that example day by day. "I can do all things through him who strengthens me" (Phil. 4:13). Human examples may inspire and challenge us, but they can't enable us to reach the heights they have reached. Jesus alone is the great empowering Example who can transform us and enable us—and He does it a day at a time. The abounding life can be ours as we trust and obey.

I was raised in the tradition of Swedish hymnody. One of my favorites, "Day by Day,"[4] reminds me of Jesus' help to live my life a day at a time and that He never fails.

Day by day, and with each passing moment, strength I find to meet my trials here;
Trusting in my Father's wise bestowment, I've no cause for worry or for fear.

He whose heart is kind beyond all measure gives unto each day what He deems best,
Lovingly its part of pain and pleasure, mingling toil with peace and rest.

Every day the Lord Himself is near me with a special mercy for each hour;
All my cares He fain would bear and cheer me, He whose name is Counselor and Power.
The protection of His child and treasure is a charge that on Himself He laid;
"As thy days, thy strength shall be in measure," — this the pledge to me He made.

Help me then, in every tribulation, so to trust Thy promises, O Lord,
That I lose not faith's sweet consolation offered me within Thy holy word.
Help me, Lord, when toil and trouble meeting, e'er to take, as from a father's hand,
One by one, the days, the moments fleeting, till I reach the promised land.

May you have the hindsight to appreciate where you have been, the foresight to anticipate where you are going, and the insight to evaluate both and make the most of your experience today. – Adapted from an Irish blessing

The landing of an eagle in the fresh snow leaves an unmistakable imprint. As we near the finish of our race, we too shall leave a mark. Our path is lighted, and the course is set for us to follow. Will our mark be that of an "eagle"?

Endnotes

1. Scott Peck, *The Road Less Traveled* (New York: Simon and Schuster, 1978), p. 15.
2. Ralph Waldo Emerson, *Society and Solitude* (New York: Cosimo, Inc., 2005), p. 20.
3. Mary A. Lathbury, "Break Thou the Bread of Life" (hymn), 1877.
4. Karolina W. Sandell-Berg, tr. A.L. Skoog, "Day by Day" (hymn), 1865.

Photo Appendix

Photo Appendix

Page 16 – A mother red fox and her kits return to the den after a round of play in the nearby forest.

Page 18 – Abundant red delicious apples hang on trees carefully pruned by master gardener Pastor Melvin Carr in East Tennessee.

Page 20 – Young bald eagles investigate the confines of their nest near Pigeon Forge, Tennessee.

Page 22 – Morning light breaks through autumn foliage at a corn crib on the Becky Cable Farmstead in Cades Cove, Tennessee.

Page 6 – The distinct profile of a bald eagle is accented against the forest shadows on Vancouver Island in British Columbia.

Page 8 – A bald eagle stretches its wings to dry and to catch the breeze off the Bering Sea in Alaska.

Page 12 – A ribbon-like trail leads through a fern colony along the crest of the Great Smoky Mountains in Tennessee.

Page 15 – Characteristic "smoke" rises from mountain ridges near Alum Cave Bluffs in the Great Smoky Mountains National Park.

Page 24 — An adult grizzly ready for its winter den shakes snow from a young spruce tree in Montana.

Page 26 — Warm rays of morning light flood an ancient sequoia grove in the High Sierra of California.

Page 30 — Buttercups and lupine adorn the Aleutian landscape of Alaska. A bald eagle waits in damp grasses to bathe in a nearby stream.

Page 32 — Rugged cliffs give way to the deep and narrow river canyon at Black Canyon of the Gunnison National Park in western Colorado.

Page 34 — The rugged coast of the Aleutian Islands near Dutch Harbor, Alaska, was the site of gun emplacements and major conflict during World War II.

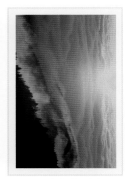

Page 36 — The sun sets over a sea of clouds from the cliff tops of Mount LeConte in Tennessee.

Page 40 — A newborn white-tailed deer fawn rests in a bed of white trillium in a Northwoods forest of the north central United States.

Page 45 — A frosty morning at Nugget Pond in Denali National Park in Alaska presents a beautiful daybreak.

Page 47 — A grey wolf pauses briefly in the foliage of autumn blueberry bushes of Minnesota as it watches the pack proceed.

Page 50 — An approaching storm allows warm light to flood the landscape at Badlands National Park in South Dakota.

Page 62 – A background of snow-capped peaks indicates the great height of a soaring bald eagle. Its scream is heard for miles in the wilderness of Alaska.

Page 64 – A female bald eagle flies swiftly and intently near the island of Adak in the Aleutian Islands of Alaska.

Page 66 – Mounting up and heading for higher elevations, a bald eagle uses great energy to break from a cliff in the Aleutian Islands of Alaska.

Page 68 – A bald eagle surveys a mountain lake, looking for fish near its surface in Unalaska, Alaska.

Page 70 – An eagle screams and soars in sub-zero temperatures above the Chilkat River near Haines, Alaska.

Page 52 – As the sun sets, casting pastel shades of light on the granite walls, Half Dome is accented above the Yosemite Valley in California.

Page 54 – A thousand beams of light break through the mist as giant sequoias stand strong in the Sequoia National Park of California.

Page 56 – A young grizzly cub waits in grasses by the Brooks River as a magpie keeps it company in Alaska's Katmai National Park.

Page 59 – Morning clouds appear as smoke signals from the tallest peaks in the Grand Teton National Park of Wyoming.

Page 60 – A bald eagle in Dutch Harbor, Alaska, surveys the view from its lofty vantage point.

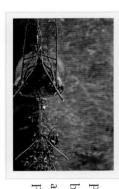

Page 74 – Grey wolves run together on a hunt in southern Ontario, Canada.

Page 78 – A beaver brings willow branches across the dam and into a pond in Alaska's Denali National Park.

Page 80 – The last light of day casts warm colors as a polar bear crosses the pack ice of Hudson Bay in Manitoba, Canada.

Page 82 – Morning light breaks on a sentinel peak in Utah's Zion National Park.

Page 84 – The photographer/author meditates on God's Word during a personal retreat in central Kentucky.

Page 86 – A bobcat looks out from a grassy shelter during a Midwestern snowstorm.

Page 88 – A grey wolf makes a noble stand in the autumn foliage of Minnesota.

Page 92 – A bald eagle walks in grasses and buttercups on a ridge top near Alaska's coast.

Page 96 – Two young grizzlies survey the vast tundra of Denali National Park in Alaska.

Page 98 – A mother polar bear and her two cubs cross the rugged pack ice of Hudson Bay in Manitoba, Canada.

Page 108 – A wilderness river tumbles through ancient boulders beneath peaking fall color in northern Wisconsin.

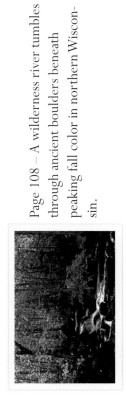

Page 110 – A peaceful lake is locked from the Bering Sea by a sandy wall near Summer Bay in Unalaska, Alaska.

Page 113 – The wing print of a bald eagle is seen distinctly in deep snows along the Kettle River of east central Minnesota.

Page 100 – A large grizzly is silhouetted against Naknek Lake in southwest Alaska.

Page 102 – A faint game trail leads across a ridge in Alaska's Denali National Park as a rainbow highlights the landscape.

Page 104 – A bed of western lupine covers the forest floor in California's Kings Canyon National Park.